D0852592

WITHDRAWN
UTSA Libraries

WITHDRAWN
UTSA Libraries

MANAGING THE SERIALS EXPLOSION

THE ISSUES FOR PUBLISHERS AND LIBRARIES

by
David C. Taylor

Knowledge Industry Publications, Inc.
White Plains, New York and London

Professional Librarian Series

Managing the Serials Explosion: The Issues for Publishers and Libraries

Library of Congress Cataloging in Publication Data

Taylor, David Carson
  Managing the serials explosion.

  (Professional librarian)
  Bibliography: p.
  Includes index.
  1. Serial publications.   2. Periodicals,
Publishing of.   I. Title.   II. Series: Professional
librarian series.
  Z692.S5T39   1982   070.5'72   82-14062
  ISBN 0-914236-94-6
  ISBN 0-914236-54-7 (pbk.)

Printed in the United States of America

Copyright © 1982 by Knowledge Industry Publications, Inc., 701 Westchester Ave., White Plains, NY 10604. Not to be reproduced in any form whatever without written permission from the publisher.

10   9   8   7   6   5   4   3   2   1

LIBRARY
The University of Texas
At San Antonio

Table of Contents

Preface

Many believe that serials are the primary cause of the rapid rise in the cost of library materials. Since 1970, subscription prices for old standard journals have gone haywire—doubling, tripling, quadrupling and more. Meanwhile, new journals with important-sounding titles appear each week at unreasonable prices. Both the general rise in subscription rates and the introduction of new journals add to the strain on library budgets.

Librarians, already battling inflation which is never adequately matched by budget increases, are especially disturbed by these rampaging subscription costs. They may be permitted to wonder if so many serials are needed and if their prices are not artificially high. Hard choices are required. Since serials cause most of the problem, one would expect that most of the cuts in a library's obligations would be applied to its subscriptions. Surprisingly, librarians have been slow to take this step, and their inability to do so may make them irrationally angry at serials. A major task of this book is to study the phenomenon of this cost rise for serials and try to understand the reactions to it in libraries.

A serial is a communication format whose arrangement between author, publisher and reader provides each with some benefits that a book cannot provide. Librarians have come along and entered into this relationship, which originally was not planned with them in mind. In some ways librarians have never become a full partner in the transaction; that is, the needs of libraries have not been fully considered by author and publisher. For some journals, however, librarians have become too important. The whole design of the serial is meant to appeal to librarians, and the serial would not exist without libraries and their subscription payments. The purchasing power of libraries has had an enormous influence on scholarly journals, a life-and-death importance for all but the largest publishers. When even a few libraries reduce their purchases, the effect on some publishers can be serious.

Some librarians have become openly resentful of serials publishers because of the cost squeeze. On the other hand, libraries' efforts to reduce expenditures have hurt the publishers and made them suspicious. Charges of cynicism, selfishness and unethical (even illegal) behavior are traded. Each group accuses the other of no longer having a true regard for the advance of scholarship and scholarly communication. What used to be a relationship of cooperation and comradeship (and still is between individual librarians and publishers) has become one of mutual suspicion and animosity between the two professions. This distrust will not be easy to break down while we are trapped by the economic problems which make each search desperately for ways to decrease expenses and increase income. What we will see is that the solutions found by publishers increase the problems for librarians and the solutions found by librarians increase the problems for publishers.

What we need are answers to the cost problems that beset both publishers and librarians. This book would be a bestseller if I could offer those answers, but unfortunately, I don't know them. Perhaps this book can make a contribution toward finding those answers by analyzing the problems from the perspective of both librarians and publishers.

Compared to books (which also, of course, contribute to cost problems) serials are poorly understood as a medium of communication. Serials are different from books. Everyone knows that, but no one seems to have analyzed the particulars of those differences. I believe the factors that make serials distinctive are connected to the roles played by people responsible for them: authors, editors, publishers, librarians, indexers and readers. The function of the serial in the communication of scholarship is especially important. Serials deserve the attention they are beginning to receive in the library literature. Moreover, serials are changing more rapidly than books.

The book is an ancient form of communication and very successful. The serial is also an old and enduring form of communication. While it has weaknesses, it also is very successful—too successful to curl up and die in the face of its new competition, the computer, as its critics assert will happen. Those librarians who may have breathed a sigh of relief at all the predictions of the serial's death have been rudely jostled by the vitality it continues to exhibit. If rate of multiplication and an appetite for money are indications of health, then the serial is far from moribund.

The serial is valuable and it is lively. Librarians will have to find ways to handle serials more efficiently, provide access to *all* serials, and do so while staying within their means. A tall order. Publishers are struggling with a similar problem: finding ways to publish serials more efficiently so that *all* significant knowledge will be disseminated, while producing enough income to meet the costs of publishing that knowledge. We will consider publishers and their search for solutions, but our primary focus will be on librarians and the solutions and partial solutions that they try.

Chapters in this book have the following plan: Chapter 1 defines a serial and explains its role in the communication of scholarship and popular information. Chapter 2 attempts to answer the questions, "Why are subscription prices rising so sharply?" and "Why are serials continuing to be started and to grow larger at a time when we can't afford the serials we already have?" Chapter 3 analyzes librarians' traditional methods for managing serials and the principles that lie behind those methods. Chapter 4 examines the various attempts by librarians to reduce the costs of serials by sharing and borrowing resources from other libraries and from other entities created by librarians for such cooperative programs. Chapter 5 describes library attempts to cut costs by automating serials management operations. Chapter 6 shifts to publishers, examining experimental new formats and offering some insights into their potential use and effects on libraries. Chapter 7 takes up some of the issues raised in earlier chapters and analyzes them in greater depth. Chapter 8 continues this analysis, focusing on implications for libraries and suggestions for action.

There are too many people to thank here for help and support—family, friends and colleagues—but I need to thank the staff of the University of North Carolina Library Science Library for their help and patience, Marcia Tuttle for ideas and encouragement, Adrienne Hickey for the carrot and stick, and Betsy for a thousand things, the least of all, typing.

David C. Taylor
July 1982

1

Introduction:
The Nature and Development of Serials

We have not always had serials. Even after the development of written communication, mankind got along perfectly well without them for centuries. Although there were many ancient forerunners, the true serial is considered to have started in the 17th century with the advent of newspapers throughout Europe and the 1665 publication of *Le Journal des Sçavans* in Paris and *Philosophical Transactions* in London. Since that time, there has been an enormous and steady growth in the number of serials, an "explosion" that may pose more of a challenge to libraries than any other phenomenon.

HOW MANY SERIALS ARE THERE?

Various authors have estimated the number of serials now being published. Price estimated in 1963 that scientific journal literature had *doubled every 15 years* since 1665.[1] The British Library Lending Division in 1965 subscribed to 26,235 titles in science and technology. Lancaster estimates that by 1977 some 50,000 scientific journals were being published.[2] Studies by King et al. and Fry and White estimate the annual growth of journals in the United States alone at about 2.6%, or about 50% in 15 years.[3]

Osborn, using data from the Library of Congress and not limiting himself to journals or scholarly periodicals, says that by 1957, 630,000 serial publications had at some time or place been published since the first printed newspaper in 1609. His estimate for 1971 was 900,000 serials, with a projected figure of 1.5 million serials by the year 2000.[4]

The implications of these figures for librarians and scholars are devastating. How can libraries afford to acquire information at this rate of increase? Their funds do not increase fast enough to make complete coverage possible. But if libraries do not acquire them, won't they be lost? Even if libraries do manage to identify, acquire, catalog and index all the important world literature, how can the scholars possibly read it all? Where does all this "knowledge" or "information" come from? Can it be all real, or is it puffed up by other factors that can be discounted, making the actual figures for significant publication much lower and more manageable than they appear to be?

Osborn's numbers are frightening enough, but I believe they understate by half, or perhaps more, the number of serials published. This view stems from a personal experience.

In 1972, I and other library staff members at the Michigan State University Library undertook a census of serials published at the University. We had been embarrassed several times by interlibrary loan requests for serials that were published locally, but that we could not identify in the library. A letter to departmental secretaries elicited staggering information: the 60 or so serials the library received were only the tip of the iceberg. Another hundred were quickly identified, and it was clear that the secretaries could increase the totals if we wanted to know absolutely everything available. It could safely be assumed that the same pattern existed in the departments that did not answer our questionnaire.

From our survey it was clear that we could triple or quadruple the number of serials we received and cataloged from the University. But the more we identified, the more trivial and ephemeral the serials became. There was no good place to stop, but it was clear that no one was interested in *all* of these publications. We did the sensible thing, of course; we abandoned the project, adding only a few of the more significant titles to the collection and ignoring the rest. But since we never identified all the serials out there, we did not know if other important ones had been overlooked. We could only hope that important publications would in due time make themselves known to us. Unfortunately, one of the ways would be through interlibrary loan requests from other libraries.

I feel certain this experience could be duplicated anywhere in the Western world. It is certainly not confined to the academic environment. Those faithfully produced membership newsletters are in our mailboxes, but they're not in public or school or academic library catalogs, and they're not in the Library of Congress or the *Union List of Serials, New Serial Titles, Ulrich's International Periodicals Directory* or any other directory. Libraries, in short, are very selective in their acquisitions: they are quite sensibly ignoring most of what is published already.

The library is somewhat like the naturalist moving through the jungle. The species he collects and identifies have eternal existence. The uncollected species flit out their beautiful or ugly but undocumented lives and as far as the world is concerned, never were. The serials not owned and cataloged by a library never enter the records and might as well never exist. For the most part, nothing important is lost. The significant serials, like large carnivores, will attract the library's attention. But it is also true that some serials that might have achieved significance never do so because no library finds them and gives them a place.

Some critics feel that libraries ought to ignore even more serials and let them dwindle into nonexistence. That issue will be discussed in the next chapter. First, it is important to know what we're talking about when we call a publication a "serial" and to understand the essential characteristics that make a difference not only to libraries handling them but to authors, readers, publishers and editors.

DEFINITION OF A SERIAL

What do the multivarious forms of serials have in common? An incredible variety of scholarly journals, mass- and special-interest consumer magazines, newspapers, newsletters, "shoppers guides," even yearbooks and almanacs—all of these and more are in a sense serials. They are so different in purpose, audience, content and publishing patterns from one another that it is difficult to emerge with any definition that will cover them all. In fact, the authorities cannot agree on a definition, or even, for that matter, a name.

In Britain, Davinson says the inclusive term is "periodical." In the United States, Osborn says it is "serial."[5] Their argument appears to be simple, but it becomes complicated. Osborn claims that the use of "serial" is more universal. Davinson, following David Grenfell, argues that "serial" is falling out of favor and the broad interpretation of "periodical" is growing. Osborn argues that most reference tools refer to serials as serials. Davinson counters with *British Union Catalogue of Periodicals* and *Ulrich's International Periodicals Directory*. Osborn cites the use of the term "serial" in the *Anglo-American Cataloguing Rules,* while Davinson counters with the International Standards Organization's 1SC/R 8 for *The Layout of Periodicals* and the American National Standards Institute's *Periodicals: Format and Arrangement*. Davinson argues that the term "periodical" is understood by the lay person and therefore is preferable. Osborn argues that because lay people think they understand it, it should be avoided; "periodical" is associated so closely with "magazine" that it is ambiguous when used as a comprehensive term, and therefore the library jargon word "serial" is more exact and unmistakable.[6] Our American experience may be showing. This book will use the term "serials."

This argument—sketched only briefly here—reminds us that writers about serials must define "serial" or "periodical" before they begin their analyses. Why is this so? It is rarely the case that treatises on the subject of books need to define "book" first. A book stands alone, but a serial is such because of its relationship to other publications, and this relationship is what must be carefully defined.

Elements of a Serial Definition

A serial is a publication reproduced in more than one copy and more than one issue. It has a common name identifying the issues, and dating or numbering to show the distinction and connection between one issue and another. It has no intended point of completion. The essential elements to this definition are:

1. Publication
2. Reproduction in more than one copy
3. Appearance more than once
4. A name or title shared by the multiple copies and issues
5. A numbering or dating system
6. Indefinite appearance

1. Publication. Memoranda may be numbered, dated and issued in several copies, but they are not publications. The writer of the memo decides who will read it. The publication is no doubt written with certain readers in mind, but it is they who decide to receive and read it. A memo is a boy beating a wasps' nest with a stick. The consequences are surprising but predictable, and the communication between the boy and wasps is private, although onlookers may become involved. A serial is an arrow shot into the air. It belongs to who finds and is interested in it.

2. Reproduction in more than one copy. One copy is a manuscript. Two or more copies are standard issues of a publication. The assumption is that the reproduction standardizes the issue so that the contents and format of one copy are the same as those of other copies of the issue.

3. Appearance more than once. The first issue may announce the intention to publish a serial, but it does not fit the definition of serial until the second issue appears, no matter how long the interval. Moreover, the second issue cannot be a revision of the first issue; that would make it an edition, and perhaps a successful textbook, but not a serial.

4. A name or title shared by the multiple copies and issues. The repetition of the name establishes the identity of the serial. Even when the title changes on the second issue, it is a serial if it calls itself "No. 2" and identifies the connection between the second title and the original title.

5. A number or dating system. The number or the date establishes the identity of the *issue.* The number does more than the date and is infinitely preferable. It establishes the relationship of one issue to the next. Having numbers five and four, one knows that no others were published in between. Having only the October and November issues, one assumes but cannot be sure that no others were published in between. With September and November issues, one has no idea at all whether an October issue was published.

6. Indefinite appearance. Another way to put this is "lack of projected date of completion." Some definitions of serials cite the intention of the publisher to continue indefinitely. I prefer not to try to read the publisher's mind. Besides, the publisher's intention is not decisive. I know of a publication intended to last four issues over a seven-month span which was still going seven years later.

The last point distinguishes between "serial" and multiple volume monograph work, or "set," in that one has a built-in completion date, the other not. The distinction may be more important to a cataloger than to the acquisitions librarian, since many sets can be purchased and received exactly like serials.

Publishers don't read our definitions and are not bound by them. They are inventive and imaginative, when taken as a class, and it may suit their purposes to create something in the border areas not anticipated by definition writers. For instance, Gale Research Co. has a three volume encyclopedia called *The Encyclopedia of Associations.* Volume 1 is the main subject listing, Volume 2 is the geographic register and Volume 3 is a quarterly supplement called *New Associations.* Anyone who examines Volume 3 will be struck by the fact that it is a serial! And the whole set is becoming more like a serial, as a new edition is now being published annually.

Why a Definition?

Definitions are hazardous. They attempt to identify a class of materials that can be distinguished from all others, and any exception will defeat the definition. The exceptions may prove that the definition has not named the essence of the material at all. Nevertheless, the definition should be helpful to our discussion, although any librarian with a few months experience with serials will be able to think of exceptions that are not quite described by it. The definition allows us to know whether Mr. Davinson's "periodicals" are the same as Mr. Osborn's "serials," so that we can know if their conversation is based on common experience and if their figures are comparable.

More important, the definition should help us consider how and why a serial is different from a book. To the reader, a serial is a publication that first of all delivers on a promise. The second issue, which follows the first after a certain amount of time, creates the expectation for a third issue to come after a similar interval and to have a similar appearance and content. Certainly that is why a deadline is such an important part of newspaper publishing. There are many advantages to regular editorial and printing deadlines, including the scheduling of printers and circulation staff, and avoiding extra work of handling customer complaints. But the most important is the creation in the reader's mind of the expectation of regular, reliable appearance.

READER EXPECTATIONS

Without referring to a copy, think about a periodical that you read regularly. You will be surprised how much you already know about the next issue to be published. For example, as a regular reader of *Newsweek* I can visualize many details without having studied it and without looking at a copy.

1. Size: A little smaller than an 8½ x 11-inch sheet—let's say 7¾ x 10 inches. Thickness is about a quarter of an inch.

2. Number of pages: Between 84 and 120.

3. Cover: Bright colors. Probably a photograph on a red background or bleeding off the page. Title typeset in a bold serif style in upper and lower case, the N about one inch high, white or yellow or red contrasting with background.

4. Contents and arrangement: National and international news. The cover story will usually relate to a big news story, but it can also be a "manufactured" story given significance by the treatment given to it. The cover story will have pictures and text covering 8 to 12 pages. It will include one or two "boxes" of a half page or so ruled off from the large story. The cover story will appear in the issue according to a rather rigid arrangement of stories in an order: international, national, business and the arts, with an occasional sports story and two or three editorial columns scattered throughout. There is always an editorial column on the page facing the inside back cover. Irritatingly, the Table of Contents page is not where it would be very easy to find: the page facing the inside front cover. It is on page 2 or 3. Page 1 is a beautiful, striking, expensive ad. Of the 100 or so pages, 20 will be full-page advertisements including back cover and inside back and front covers. On the pages toward the back, ads will occupy one-third of the page on the outside of the page flanking the text and black and white photos accompanying the text. Contents of these ads are predictable. They will advertise automobiles, whiskey, cigarettes, hi fidelity equipment, television sets and cameras.

Other features come easily to mind. With a little concentration any reader could describe a periodical he scans regularly in similar detail. With confidence we can predict that future issues will follow the same patterns, with only minor changes, as long as the periodical is successful.

Readers will read one periodical for entertainment, others for news, others for professional or scholarly information. Because they know basically what to expect, they do not have to decide what to read or where to go to find this reading. Of course, the issues they read will have to contain new information put in interesting or otherwise valuable ways, but the new and different will be entirely within the bounds of the expected.

AUTHORS AND READERS

To authors, the serial supplies a regular and receptive audience. Since the readers of a serial expect certain kinds of articles, they are a self-selected audience *expecting* and *wanting* those kinds of articles; and the serial they read becomes the most efficient vehicle for *reaching* people who expect and want those kinds of articles. By publishing *Popular Photography,* the publisher not only caters to photographers, but creates new photographers; that is, people who *need more information about photography.*

For the author the serial has the additional advantage of being quicker than book publication. (There are exceptions. Some scholarly journals have 18-month backlogs, while some book publishers have developed extremely fast publication.) Moreover, writing an article usually requires less investment of the author's own time than would a book.

For scholarly writers the article may represent an experiment or observation too short for book-length treatment. Often the scholar's reputation and real contribution to his field is made through journal articles. Late in his career he may begin writing books based on his life's work, summarizing and synthesizing the findings already published in journals.

The scholar's journal readers are extremely important. They establish the prestige of the author and by their feedback (letters, conversations) and other reactions (citations and quotations) give their stamp of approval. But whether anyone reads it or not, the publication in the journal provides documentation of the work. This simultaneously establishes precedence and makes it available to other scholars.

The library expands but diffuses the audience for serials. As the number of serials has grown, the role of the library has become more important. No one can afford to subscribe to all the serials he would like to read. Instead, we subscribe to a few, and depend upon the library to provide us access to the rest. Most who read library copies will not read them as soon after publication as will personal subscribers. In fact, this time dimension is extremely important. Personal copies are lost, misplaced, discarded, disorganized. Library copies are permanent. The documentation that the scholar needs is possible because of the permanence of library copies. A creative work or an important bit of knowledge is available through the ages as long as we can keep our libraries functioning.

The library as subscriber also has become important as a market to serial publishers. *Newsweek* editors would not be happy to lose 40,000 or so library subscriptions, but with 3 million other subscribers it could get along without libraries. That is no longer true of almost any scholarly journal. Some sell to almost no individuals. Some have thousands of individual subscribers, but even these need library subscriptions to survive because of the costs of publishing today.

A BRIEF HISTORY OF SERIALS

Although a detailed historical treatment of serials is well beyond the scope of this book, a brief look at the development of modern serials from their early antecedents may be useful to an understanding of current issues.

Newspapers and Newsletters

An early precursor of the serial was the daily publication of the proceedings of the senate and the plebeians during the Consulship of Julius Caesar in the 5th century B.C. This written record, which was posted in a public place, included not only legislative proceedings, but political affairs, news of the emperor and his family and other noteworthy events. Although the senate portion of the proceedings was later eliminated the "publication" continued until Constantine moved the center of political authority in the Roman Empire from Rome to Constantinople in A.D. 330. Called by various names—*acta diurna, acta populi* and *acta publica*—this daily message board was, except for printing, circulation and comic strips, a newspaper every bit as much as *The Washington Post.*

Another early and long-lasting forerunner to the serial was *Ti-pao,* a handwritten paper begun in China during the Han dynasty (206 B.C. to A.D. 220). It continued through the era of block printing in China and into the era of printing from movable type. When it ended in 1736 it was succeeded by another title, *Ching-pao.* When did it become a serial? When it was reproduced in multiple copies? One could say so and yet, it was almost a serial for centuries before that. When the amanuensis put down his brush, *Ti-pao* probably can be said to have become the first true serial. Ironically, at the same time it created one of the first technologically displaced men. It is also of passing interest that this most venerable title exhibited at its demise that curse of the serials librarian, the "cease-and-supersede."

That amazing phenomenon, the newsletter, one of the most distinctive features of 20th century publication, is also very old in concept. Medieval and Renaissance mercantile companies had a large appetite for specific news on prices, travel conditions, taxes, etc. From the 13th century on, these companies gathered news through series of handwritten letters from far-flung correspondents. One outstanding collection of correspondence from the Fugger house, a family mercantile company, is now in the National Library in Vienna. It consists of 17,600 letters covering 35,230 pages between the years 1568 and 1605.

Meanwhile, printed newsbooks had begun to appear. The earliest known example in England was a small pamphlet printed in 1513 by Richard Fawkes called *The Trew Encoun-*

tre, a report of the battle of Flodden Field. Some regularly appearing newsbooks in Strasbourg and Basel began to be numbered by 1566 and thus made the transition from books to series. Yearly, half-yearly and even monthly summaries of the news began to appear. *Mercurius Gallobelgicus,* one of the more noteworthy early news summaries, was published from 1594 to 1635.

Inexorably, these developments in information dissemination ingenuity led to true newspapers in the first decade of the 17th century. *Nieuwe Tijdinghen* was published in Antwerp from 1605 on by Abraham Verhoeven. It, like other newspapers, was distinguished by unspecialized subject matter, with ties to a locality, by somewhat regular appearance and by its development from badly circulated commercial bulletins and newsletters. By 1640 almost all the countries in Europe had one or more newspapers.

In America, pamphlets and broadsides were forerunners of the first newspaper: the rather seedy *Publick Occurrences Both Foreign and Domestic in Boston,* published by Benjamin Harris in 1690. It was quickly suppressed by the authorities because of an embarrassing reference to the massacre of French captives by Indians allied to the British. John Campbell, Boston's postmaster, brought out the next newspaper, the *Boston News-Letter* in 1704. It was basically a dull rehash of stale news lifted from foreign newspapers. Benjamin Franklin's brother James was the first newspaper publisher qualified by education and writing ability to publish a newspaper. His *New-England Courant* began in 1719. Benjamin showed his genius for newspaper writing and editing as an apprentice, and set up his own famous printing shop and newspaper in Philadelphia in 1729.[7]

Scholarly Journals

Other types of serials developed in Europe in the 17th century. The needs of scientists to communicate their discoveries and observations led to voluminous correspondence. Each scholar wrote to his fellows and replied to those who wrote to him. Science was a participation sport, open to any learned gentlemen. But the communication needed to be organized. In 1665 the *Journal des Sçavans,* a weekly publication put together by Denis de Sallo, appeared in Paris. Considered the first true scholarly journal, it consisted of lists of new books published with some annotations on contents and scope, obituaries, scientific discoveries and inventions, court decisions and current events. Until it was suspended in 1792 the preponderance of its pages was devoted to the lists and reviews of books. When it resumed in 1816, its title was *Journal des Savants,*[8] an updated spelling of "Sçavans."

The year 1665 also saw the first monthly issue of *Philosophical Transactions: giving some account of the present Undertakings, Studies, and Labours of the Ingenious in many considerable parts of the World.* While officially the organ of the Royal Society of London, it was owned by its editor, Henry Oldenburg. Not until 1753 did the Society take full charge of the *Transactions,* selecting papers for publication from those read before its members. The Society's statutes provided for a record to be kept of "observations, histories, and discourses of natural and artificial things—as also such philosophical experiments, together with particular accounts of their process. . ."[9]

I like to imagine the librarian at the Bodleian Library in Oxford receiving the first issue of *Philosophical Transactions* in March 1665 with great displeasure. "What, another journal?

What purpose can possibly be served by another scholarly periodical when we already have one!"

Other scholarly journals soon followed. Francesco Nazzari began the *Giornale dei letterati* in Italy in 1668. *Acta Eruditorum Lipsiensium* appeared in Germany in 1682. By 1699, 20 scholarly journals were being published in Europe.

In the United States, the *Medical Repository,* published in New York from 1797 to 1824, was the first periodical that could be called a learned journal. It devoted much of its space to the study of yellow fever and other epidemic diseases, but also published observations of natural history, physical geography, chemistry, mineralogy and meteorology. Medical journals soon proliferated. In 1820 the *Philadelphia Journal of Medical and Physical Sciences* was founded, becoming in 1827 the *American Journal of the Medical Sciences.* It still continues, as does the *American Journal of Science,* begun in New Haven as the *American Journal of Science and Arts* in 1818.[10]

Popular Journals

The proliferation of periodicals in Europe did not stop with scholarly journals. In 1691 there appeared a more popular and vocational title, *Collection for the Improvement of Husbandry and Trade.* It was an ancestor in spirit to *Botanical Magazine* (1786) and to many 19th century periodicals associated with the Mechanics Institute movement. In *Popular Science, Popular Mechanics, Popular Electronics, Organic Gardening* and many similar titles today, we recognize the same type of periodical.

Another development was the appearance of periodicals designed specifically for entertainment. The French *Mercure Gallant* began in 1672, followed by a German periodical in 1688 and by *Athenian Gazette* in London in 1690. *Gentleman's Journal* and *Ladies' Mercury* followed in 1692. Some noteworthy journals that appeared in the next 50 years in England are the *Review* (1702), *Tatler* (1709), *Spectator* (1711), *Gentleman's Magazine* (1731) and *Scots Magazine* (1739). During this period works of some of the greatest writers were published in periodicals: Daniel Defoe, Richard Steele, Joseph Addison, Samuel Johnson and James Boswell. The popular press designed for a female audience flourished at this time, too. In addition to *Ladies' Mercury,* there were *The Female Tatler* (1709), *The Female Spectator* (1744), *Ladies Magazine* (1749) and a later and better *Ladies Magazine* (1770).

Literary, political and some scientific articles were included in early general magazines published in America from 1741 on. Most of these earlier efforts were short-lived because of the difficulties the pioneer editors and publishers had finding writers of original material, inducing subscribers to pay up, and distributing the periodicals before the Postal Service began to provide cheap and dependable service.

Critical Reviews

Journals devoted to critical reviews started with the *Edinburgh Review* in 1802. It was soon followed by imitators: *Quarterly Review* (1809), *Blackwoods Magazine* (earlier title *Blackwood's Edinburgh Magazine,* 1817), *Athenaeum* (1826), *Westminster Review* (1824), *Spectator* (1828), *Bentley's Miscellany* (1837) and *Cornhill Magazine* (1848). *Cornhill,* edited by Thackeray, increased its emphasis on fiction, and apparently found the successful formula. It was the first periodical to circulate 100,000 copies of an issue. This accomplishment was also an indication of the increasing audience—a rising middle class with a hunger for reading, the ability to buy periodicals and a distribution system able to handle them.[11]

Almanacs and Yearbooks

There are two kinds of serials that are also books: almanacs and yearbooks.

Almanacs are older than newspapers or periodicals. The earliest known issue of *Le Compost et Kalendrier des Bergiers* was published in Paris in 1480. Kronick says:

> [The almanac] is among the earliest publications of a popular nature to come from the new mechanized printing process. It was hawked throughout the countryside by colporteurs. It was a veritable encyclopedia of information for the countryman, including a calendar for each month listing the feast-days, along with hygienic and other kinds of advice. It also included the standard "zodiac man" which recommended the appropriate time for various kinds of treatments, as well as the familiar blood-letting manikin which illustrated the various body sites to apply the lancet.[12]

Most of the early almanacs were published by physicians and were distinguished by careful instructions to lay persons about the days and hours on which it would be propitious to be bathed or bled. Almanacs seem to have been associated with astrology and may have been an outgrowth of annual publications of pamphlets that properly should be called calendars. They contained little beyond the dates and apparently were intended to be thrown away when the year was over. Some of these publications actually predate printing. Almanacs in the 17th and 18th centuries also were aimed at farmers, with instructions on food storage methods, planting times and other advice.

Interestingly, almanacs have never been a vehicle for the publication of scholarly information. They have been and still are a vehicle for popularized scientific information, practical advice and amusement. Benjamin Franklin was an esteemed scientist, but his *Poor Richard's Almanack* is not remembered for any scientific observations but for aphorisms and practical homespun advice: "Early to bed and early to rise, makes a man healthy, wealthy, and wise," and "fish and visitors stink in three days."[13]

The yearbook is another early form of annual publication. The best example is undoubtedly one of the earliest, the *Annual Register*, begun in 1759 in England as a history of the year 1758. James Dodsley apologized in the preface that his new periodical was not a weighty work of erudition, but hoped that with the admixture of some humor, variety and good writing, his efforts would "imperceptibly insinuate a taste of knowledge, and in some measure gratify that taste."[14]

The arrangement of each volume stayed remarkably close to his plan for years. First there is an account of world events, focusing on but not limited to English interests; a chronicle of domestic news, centering on the royalty's doings; and a section of state papers, including speeches, diplomatic correspondence and treaties. (The 1776 volume has the Declaration of

Independence, the 1793 volume the abstract of the new French Constitution, and so forth.) Other sections include biography ("Characters"), natural history, miscellaneous essays, poetry and book reviews. Through the years with different editors and new publishers, the format stayed the same and the writing even-handed in treating the affairs of nations. However, by 1863 the poetry and essays had disappeared and the historical portions had taken over all the pages. The 1978 edition has pictures, but otherwise has strayed very little from the original conception 220 years before.

MODERN DEVELOPMENTS

As shown by the brief survey above, most modern serials have roots in ancient times. An examination of their continuing development is not the purpose of this book, but we can make a few generalizations here about their growth and future prospects.

Newspapers, Journals and Magazines

Newspapers have proliferated all over the world in cities, towns, universities and hamlets. While newspapers have appeared to grow little in the last 40 years in England and the United States, those in the underdeveloped countries have offset that stagnancy with the vitality that comes from burgeoning nationhood and hope, and a growing educated populace. Scholarly journals have continued to grow in numbers, in pages, in subjects and specialties covered—and in costs.

Popular journals have had their ups and downs, with well-publicized deaths of 20th century giants like *Life, Look, Colliers, Pageant* and *The Saturday Evening Post.* But three have been born for every one that died, and *Life* and *The Saturday Evening Post* have been reborn. The deaths occur as periodicals lose their ability to meet competition, attract advertisers and anticipate changing reader habits. But the new hopefuls take their place, and some find the audience, advertisers and writers needed for success.

Photography and color printing have continued to widen the appeal and make the potential audience greater for popular magazines. Specialization is one formula that has caught on, as sports magazines, modelers' magazines, travel magazines, "men's magazines," news magazines and others all find stable audiences and compete with other similar publications.

Newsletters

In the last 60 years the newsletter, of such importance in medieval Europe, has developed a fantastic new life in the U.S. Some of the most successful offer inside information on investments and government activities. *The Kiplinger Letter* began the modern trend in 1923 and still has perhaps the highest circulation (350,000) of the newsletters, but some of the most interesting publications now make their money with very high subscription rates to a very few subscribers. Examples are the Bureau of National Affairs' *Daily Report for Executives,* at $2385 a year, and Danielle Hunebelle's *International Letter*, at $3600 a year ($75 per page). What they sell is knowledge that few have access to, transmitted swiftly and in an easy-to-read format.

Another 20th century newsletter phenomenon may be as remarkable as the expensive financial advice newsletter. This is the lowly, common membership newsletter. It is everywhere: church, union, corporation, and professional, regional, local, national, school, alumni, booster, civic groups. Almost any organization that has a small treasury and volunteer officers can produce a newsletter by the inexpensive reproduction processes now available. Many are mimeographed or photocopied, others produced by moderately priced offset printing. Any American child who has reached the age of 18 since 1970 and never seen his name in print has truly been deprived.

New Kinds of Serials

"Monographs in series" are apparently a rather late development. This kind of series (for instance, the *Loeb Classical Library* which began in 1912) is the hybrid that is both serial and not serial. Each volume stands alone as a book and can be purchased and read as a book without reference to any other volume in the series. Yet the numbering and series title may help the publisher develop individual volumes, strengthen the sales of weaker volumes in the series, and enable libraries to purchase all the volumes automatically on a "standing order." That is, the volume is shipped and invoiced when ready, the library having agreed ahead of time to accept it and pay for it. In fact, some monographs in series might not exist without libraries to buy them on standing order.

We now have the free periodical. Many of these are "house-organs," the slick product of a large public relations-conscious corporation. Others are "controlled circulation" periodicals, advertising vehicles paid for entirely by the ads, not the subscribers. The mailing lists for these publications are carefully scrutinized and rigorously weeded of those who would not be in a position to pay for the goods and services advertised. It can be very difficult for a library or a private individual to acquire controlled circulation periodicals, even when the articles published in them are of great interest, or the information essential.

Second class mailing regulations of the U.S. Postal Service have created another class of serial that could be called the pseudo-periodical. The regulations require that a publication appear regularly three times a year or more. Many a university discovered that its catalog could be mailed much more cheaply if it were considered a number in a series that is published monthly or quarterly. Consequently a monthly series may be invented called the "Information Bulletin Series." Bulletins 3 and 7 each year may be summer and regular catalogs of the university. Number 1 may be the president's annual report, and the other nine issues may be alumni bulletins and the like.

Another new phenomenon is the "shoppers guide," a free collection of advertising with a minimum of editorial content, if any. These may be delivered door to door or distributed at retail counters or in newspaper vending boxes in malls and on street corners on a weekly basis.

New Forms of Publication

One of the most widely discussed publishing phenomena of the 20th century is the potential replacement of print-on-paper publications by alternative media. Electronic publishing, in which information is generated and accessed via computer, may mean the death of the printed journal, according to some analysts. One of the best known proponents of this view is F.W. Lancaster, who conceives of "a paperless information system of the future—let us say, in the year 2001. In this system, professionals in all fields of human activity will use electronic communications and storage in place of the generation, transmission, storage and destruction of billions of pieces of paper."[15]

Although many forecasters disagree with this belief in an all-electronic communications world of the near future, there is no doubt that computer and telecommunications technologies are already making electronic publication feasible for some serials. Many impediments remain—economic, technological, social—but the "electronic revolution" that is transforming so much of contemporary life will almost certainly have a growing and profound impact on serials publication. Electronic publication and its effect on libraries will be discussed further in Chapters 6 and 7.

One alternative to print-on-paper that has become widely accepted is the micrographic serial. Since 1938, with the formation of University Microfilms, printed serials have been filmed as an alternative to binding or as a means of preserving material which was deteriorating. Since the mid-1960s, when *Wildlife Diseases* began to appear on microfilm, some journals have been produced on microform as *the* means of publication. Today many scholarly publishers, including the American Chemical Society, make journals available to subscribers in print and film formats. Microform format is also used by the National Technical Information Service and the Educational Resources Information Clearinghouse in their large-scale publishing activities.

CONCLUSIONS

While most modern serials have ancient forbears, some of the developments in the 20th century are unique. Over all, the variety and sheer numbers of serials being published in the United States today are sometimes bewildering, but they also indicate the vitality of serials publishing.

However, both libraries and publishers are beset by a cost squeeze. The costs of publication—for paper, printing, postage, salaries, rent, etc.—have risen dramatically in the past 10 years. To stay in business, publishers must charge higher subscription rates. At the same time, library budgets are shrinking and cannot keep up with the increased costs of materials, salaries, supplies, building maintenance, and so forth. Proposition 13 has threatened the ability of state and local governments to collect taxes for a variety of services, including library services.

Academic enrollments are expected to decrease as the last year of the baby boom generation graduates. If enrollment does decline, tuition income, private donations, and state and federal government support may follow suit. Academic library budgets will probably go down at the same rate as the total college and university budgets go down. How will librarians adjust to these changed circumstances?

Librarians so far have reacted to restricted budgets by cutting book purchases and serial subscriptions. These cuts have sent shock waves through the publishing community. Librarians have been forced to rethink the library's purpose and streamline library procedures. Librarians have been forced to be more selective in choosing the materials that enter the collection. Librarians have been forced to learn more about how readers actually use books and serials in order to be able to make better choices. Librarians, like publishers, are considering new technologies and new schemes of cooperation in order to achieve their purposes at lower costs. The problems of libraries and publishers, and their attempts to solve them, will be examined in the following chapters.

FOOTNOTES

1. Derek DeSolla Price, *Little Science, Big Science* 1963 (New York: Columbia University Press, 1963), p. 8.

2. F.W. Lancaster, *Toward Paperless Information Systems* (New York: Academic Press, 1978), p. 66.

3. D.W. King et al., *Statistical Indicators of Scientific and Technical Communication* (1960-1980), vol. 2, (Rockville, MD: King Research, 1976), p. 124; and Bernard M. Fry and Herbert S. White *Economics and Interaction of the Publisher-Library Relationship in the Production and Use of Scholarly and Research Journals,* U.S. National Science Foundation Office of Science Information Service, 1975, (NTIS PB 249 108) p. 173.

4. Andrew W. Osborn, *Serial Publications, Their Place and Treatment in Libraries,* 3rd ed., (Chicago: American Library Association, 1980), pp. 24-25.

5. D.E. Davinson, *The Periodicals Collection,* rev. and enl. ed., (London: A. Deutsch, 1978), pp. 7-12; and Osborn, *Serial Publications,* pp. 15-16.

6. Osborn, *Serial Publications,* p. 16.

7. John Tebbel, *The Compact History of the American Newspaper* (New York: Hawthorne Books, 1963), pp. 11-21.

8. David A. Kronick, *A History of Scientific and Technical Periodicals; The Origins and Development of the Scientific and Technical Press 1665-1790,* 2nd ed., (Metuchen, NJ: Scarecrow Press, 1976), pp. 77-78.

9. Martha Ornstein, *The Role of Scientific Societies in the Seventeenth Century,* 3rd ed., (Chicago: University of Chicago Press, 1938), p. 109.

10. Cf. James Luther Mott, *A History of American Magazines 1741-1850,* (Cambridge: Harvard University Press, 1957), vol. 1.

11. Davinson, *Periodicals Collection,* pp. 23-24.

12. Kronick, *Scientific and Technical Periodicals,* p. 233.

13. Benjamin Franklin, *Poor Richard: The Almanacks for the Years 1733-1758* (New York: The Heritage Press, 1964), pp. 32, 37.

14. *The Annual Register, or a View of History, Politicks and Literature, for the Year 1758,* (1759), pp. v, vi.

15. F.W. Lancaster, "The Future of the Library in the Age of Telecommunications," *Telecommunications and Libraries: A Primer for Librarians and Information Managers,* (White Plains, NY: Knowledge Industry Publications, Inc., 1981), p. 146.

2

The High Cost of Serials

The rising cost of serials may have been the single factor with the greatest effect on academic libraries in the last 10 years. It has forced libraries to reexamine their basic acquisition activities and goals, and their relationships to other libraries. It has certainly introduced more hate than love into their love-hate relationship with publishers.

Why have the costs of serials to libraries risen so dramatically in the past decade? The answer is twofold: the increase in subscription prices and the increase in the number of journals (and other periodicals) being published, creating pressure on libraries to buy more and more. This chapter will consider both aspects of the problem.

Are publishers making enormous profits at the expense of libraries, or do the jacked-up subscription rates truly represent the costs of publishing? Do we really need all—or even a large percentage—of the serials now available? To answer these questions we will examine some of the financial problems that beset both libraries and publishers; the different kinds of serials and their publishers; and serials readership.

SUBSCRIPTION RATES

According to the 1981 price index for serials in the U.S. the average annual subscription price of 3425 journals was $39.13 in 1981, an increase of 13.3% over 1980. The increase the previous year was 13.7%. For five years, from 1976 to 1981, the price rose 73.8%![1]

Subscriptions have eaten up so much of the library budget that no library has been able to absorb the costs easily, no matter how well off financially it is. In fact, some of the larger libraries have been affected most, because of their larger commitment to serials.

R.H. Blackburn, Chief Librarian of the University of Toronto succinctly stated the problem. In his 1975-76 annual report, he wrote:

> The steady upward trend in the price of books and journals in the international market in which we must buy has amounted to at least a doubling in the past six years. In the last year, for instance, the average price of our subscriptions rose 16.4% to $35.93, and we were paying for 20,713 of them. Since our budget for purchases has remained fairly fixed in dollar amounts,

our purchasing power has dropped by more than half, though the total volume of scientific and scholarly publishing continues to go up. Moreover, our standing commitments which involve recurring costs year after year (subscription renewals, continuations, standing orders for currently published books, binding, shipping and insurance) take a share which has risen from 42% in 1968-69 to 72% in 1975-76 (and 83% in 1976-77) so that there is little money left for anything else. . . The purchasing power of the "discretionary" part of the book budget has sunk in eight years to only 14% of what it was in 1968-69.[2]

Library Subscription Budgets

In the past decade many libraries have discovered a mechanism at work in their libraries that few noticed before. When the price of library materials goes up faster than the library budget, an increasing proportion of money will be spent on serials and a decreasing proportion on monographs. When this tendency repeats itself year after year, the shift in funds can be ruinous to established acquisitions programs.

According to the statistics reported to the Association of Research Libraries (ARL), the University of Toronto cut its subscriptions from 47,866 in 1975-76 to 42,244 in 1979-80.[3] Nevertheless, the subscription budget doubled from $750,057 in 1975-76 to $1,546,564 in 1979-80. The proportion of acquisitions funds spent on subscriptions jumped from 24.1% to 46.7%.

ARL's statistics reveal that other libraries are experiencing similar problems. Texas A&M's spending on subscriptions went from $270,000 (19.7%) in 1975-76 to $904,190 (54.5%) in 1979-80. Syracuse University spent 27% of its acquisitions funds on subscriptions in 1975-76, and 60% in 1979-80. Temple University went from 25% on subscriptions in 1975-76 to 62.8% in 1979-80. Massachusetts Institute of Technology's (MIT) spending jumped from $481,918 in 1975-76 to $834,307 in 1979-80 and only maintained subscriptions in the 60% range by adding $438,000 in total funds between those years. None of these libraries decreased its subscriptions but none added substantially to them.

Case Western Reserve University cut its subscriptions by 651 and added $200,000 to its budget (+27%) but its subscription costs rose 76%, despite the cancellations. The subscriptions share of the Case Western library acquisitions budget rose from 58.7% to 81.6%! The amount of money available for the purchase of books fell from $309,002 to $174,957.

According to the 1980-81 ARL statistics, spending by university libraries for serials increased 13.8% per year from 1976 to 1981. Spending for books and other nonserials only increased 4.2% per year over that period.[4]

Trying To Keep Up with Inflation

Libraries faced with these budget shortfalls have desperately sought larger increases in order to keep up with the inflation in costs of library materials. In his annual report for 1979-80, Dr. Blackburn reports the bad news that despite an effort by the university to maintain the library's book purchasing power, the 11% increase for 1980-81 would not meet the inflation of book and journal prices. As he analyzes the problem:

> The situation is extremely critical because about 84% of the book fund is committed before the year even begins, to subscriptions, standing orders, continuations, binding, and shipping charges. This leaves only 16% to buy books for the reference collections and special collections of all kinds . . . for the local libraries in 15 faculties and teaching departments, for all research items which are outside the scope of our standing orders . . . and for covering unexpected rises of price. . . . This 16%, and everything that depends on it, could be virtually wiped out by one year's inflation.[5]

Most of the academic libraries in North America have experienced a similar loss in buying power and the squeezing of the acquisition budget by subscription and standing order commitments. Few university administrations can afford to increase library budgets enough to provide cost-of-living increases to personnel, keep up with inflationary increases in equipment and supplies, and provide funds to keep up with more-than-inflationary book and periodical prices.

Those who can may be self-defeating, says Richard DeGennaro in the most important single article written on this subject. "Up to now, our standard response to the problem of escalating journal prices has been to plead and beg for higher budgets from our funding authorities, for subsidies from the government, and for grants from foundations. All these and more are desperately needed, but this kind of help is certain to come too little and too late. And when such help comes, it will only encourage publishers to raise the institutional subscription rates even higher, and to publish more unnecessary, largely unread journals."[6]

In this call to action, DeGennaro accuses publishers of treating libraries as a captive audience, and increasing journal prices as much as the traffic will bear. He also claims publishers create new, specialized journals at low cost to themselves but at high cost to libraries who must buy them at inflated institutional subscription rates. He implies further that publishers used to consider themselves part of the scholarly enterprise, but that the inflation of the 1970s has created a different climate, making journal publishing an opportunity for profit and that the unquestioning slow-to-cancel libraries are targets of that opportunity. Even learned societies used inflated subscription rates to subsidize membership services.[7]

DeGennaro is easy to quote because he writes clearly and provocatively. He accuses faculty members of using journals as vehicles for self-promotion, not scholarship.[8] He accuses librarians of being illogically wed to the desire to have complete runs, and urges them to wake up and cancel the serials that sit unread.[9] If he is right, there is little possibility of dialogue between librarians and publishers. I think that much of what he says is true, but in general, he is wrong. I believe publishers and librarians have to stop being angry at each other if they are to solve their mutual problems.

THE COST SQUEEZE FOR PUBLISHERS

Librarians should understand that scholarly publishers have enormous problems. They have explored all possible means of improving income for their journals. They have gone to great lengths to reduce expenses for their journals. Still, the costs go up—15%, 20%, 30% a year.

Advertising Revenues

Publishers have gone after advertising revenue, an income producer that American journals have tapped successfully for many years. In 1898 the American Chemical Society (ACS) received $620.77 from subscriptions, $649.96 from advertising and $6490 from dues. In 1900 it received $917.29 from subscriptions, $1129.50 from ads and $7500 from dues. In 1930 the figures had grown to $167,000 in advertising and $294,000 in dues and subscriptions.[10] In recent years, the advertising dollar has risen greatly, but total income needs have risen still more—and advertising revenue has provided a smaller percentage of that income. In 1972 the ACS took in $3 million in member and nonmember subscriptions, and only $900,000 through advertising.[11] By 1981, income from printed publications and dues reached $47 million; from advertising, $6 million. To put these raw numbers in perspective, note that advertising was 9% of subscriptions and dues in 1890, 13% in 1900, 56% in 1930, 26% in 1972, and back to 13% in 1981.[12]

This trend in advertising income for the ACS is consistent with that for other scholarly publishers. The Fry-White study, mentioned in Chapter 1, showed that advertising revenue, while a significant source of income for many types of publishers, declined in importance on the average for all categories of publishers (commercial, society, university press and other not-for-profit publishers) and for all subject disciplines (pure science, applied science and technology, humanities and social sciences) between 1969 and 1973. While advertising revenues went up for all categories except science journals between 1969 and 1973, it did not go up as much as total revenues (and costs) for any of the categories. Despite attempts by many publishers to increase advertising revenue, the income from this source has not been as great as hoped because advertisers are not terribly interested.[13] They know that researchers go from indexes to the specific articles wanted and do not linger over the ads.[14] In fact, advertising income for scientific and technical journals is almost negligible. Magazines do much better, but journals do poorly.[15]

Page Charges

Other sources of income to supplement subscriptions have also been tapped by publishers. Society publishers of journals in pure science have been able to achieve a great deal of income from "page charges," a form of subsidy by authors. S.A. Goudsmit of the American Physical Society (APS) estimated in 1968 that 70% of the publication costs of the *Physical Review* and *Physical Review Letters* were met by page charges, only 30% by subscriptions.[16] This has changed considerably in recent years.

According to Marjorie Scal of Cambridge University Press, page charges in the early 1960s were generally paid under the same grants that supported the original research. The National Science Foundation (NSF) announced in 1961 that federal research grants would include page charges for scientific journals, since publication of research results was a legitimate and necessary part of the research. However, in the late 1960s and early 1970s the trend began to reverse, as federal government subsidies of scientific research began to decline. Foreign authors and authors working on their own, not on grants, were unable to pay the charges. As journals experienced more and more difficulty in collecting page charges, they increased charges for authors' reprints or subscription prices significantly.[17]

The authors of *Scholarly Communication* describe the history and significance of the page charge.

> Page charges were initiated by the *Physical Review* about 1932 at $2 per published page and have risen to more than $70 a page. The rationale for the page charge, which was set to cover editorial and composition costs, was the belief that research is not complete until it is published. Subscription costs were kept low because they had to cover only the costs of production, primarily paper and press work, and distribution costs. Page charges were always assessed against the author's institution, not the author. The system worked well as long as research was well funded. When budgets tightened, payments for page charges declined precipitously. Many journals in the sciences then introduced the two-track system—relatively rapid publication (within six months) for those who paid, and delayed publication (up to two years), for those who did not.[18]

Because of the changes in the federal government's funding of research, the page charge has almost completely died out now as a significant source of income for most journal publishers.

Subsidies

Subsidies never appear to have been a major source of funds for scholarly journals but that doesn't mean publishers haven't tried. Most foundations have shunned grant requests from journal publishers, although the same foundations may issue grants to authors while they are writing books. Many scholarly journals do enjoy the indirect subsidies of universities. Those journals based at universities usually do not pay rent, the secretarial expense may be paid by the institution, and the professor who gives his or her time to editing duties may be relieved of some instruction hours or other committee assignments.

When a society budgets a certain amount from its dues income for subscriptions for members, that cannot properly be called subsidy. In fact, that budget almost never amounts to the same price per member subscription as nonmembers pay, so it could be considered a subsidy of the society by the journal!

Back Issues and Reprints

Most scholarly publishers realize some money from the sale of back issues. The study by Machlup, Leeson and Associates in 1974 showed that 2.2% of the income of 137 journals studied was from back issue sales.[19] The figure reported for the ACS journals for 1972 was $200,000, or 3.2%, but by 1981 back issue sales had dropped to $100,000, or .22% (.0022)![20]

The sale of reprints is a better source of income than back issues for the ACS: $550,000, or 8.7% of its income, in 1972 and $1 million, or 2.2% in 1981.[21] The journals studied by Macklup, Leeson and Associates received 4.8% of their income from reprints.[22] Probably most reprints are sold to authors in lieu of or in addition to page charges.

Reprints are a sore point between publishers and libraries. Publishers have been convinced for years that libraries illegally photocopy articles from journals and that this systematic copying robs them of subscription and reprint income. Many of them fully expected that the new copyright law of 1976 would stop this "unfair practice" by libraries. So far the copyright law has not made a substantial difference. The Association of American Publishers (AAP) and the Information Industry Association (IIA) formed the Copyright Clearance Center to handle requests for photocopying and to receive and distribute royalties. Receipts have been disappointing. To publishers this indicates that there is widespread infringement of the law. To librarians it indicates what they have been saying all along: that the massive photocopying in libraries is done by the public, not librarians, and is not and never has been illegal. The two points of view differ widely and do not show much movement toward a mutual understanding. We will deal more extensively with photocopying and subscriptions and royalties in Chapter 4. Suffice it to say now that there does not appear to be any immediate improvement in income for publishers from this source.

Cost Hikes for Publishers

As the foregoing discussion shows, all the sources of income are closed or limited to publishers except subscription fees. Meanwhile the costs of producing a journal have increased rapidly. The price of paper more than doubled between 1970 and 1980. Nelson W. Polsby, managing editor of the *American Political Science Review,* reported that the cost per issue had gone up from $.89 a copy in June 1970 to $1.52 in June 1975, and the 1970 issue had 388 pages to 312 for the 1975 issue.[23] That's 10 pages for 2.3 cents in 1970, and 10 pages for 4.9 cents in 1975, an increase of 112.4% in five years. During those same five years the consumer price index went up only 38.6%.[24]

The price of paper is just one example of the tremendous increase in the cost of doing business as a publisher. Number 3 uncoated book paper, a standard high grade paper used widely in publishing, has increased in cost at a steady rate of 9.3% since 1972. Rolls of paper that cost $307 a tone and sheet paper that cost $356 a tone in 1972 cost $480 and $555, respectively, in 1977 and $747 and $867, respectively, in 1982, according to Stewart Furlong, president of the book paper division of the WWF Paper Corporation of Bala Cynwyd, PA.*

Printing costs have risen at least as fast, postage even faster. Salaries and wages, rent, telephone rates, and all other costs have matched the cost-of-living increases or exceeded them. Publishers must show a profit to survive. If costs cannot be kept down, income will have to match them or the publisher must go out of business.

Where is the increased revenue to come from? Payments from readers. How can publishers expand this income? There appears to be little market for additional subscribers. Even though many publishers have been able to increase their sales abroad, total sales for scholarly journals appear to be down.

Two recent reports corroborate a general decline in circulation of scholarly journals. In a paper given before the Second International Conference of Scientific Editors, in October 1980, Chomet and Nejman reported on a study of circulation and income figures for physics

---

*Personal communication with author, June 1982.

journals. They concluded that most of them had experienced an initial rapid rise in subscriptions for four or five years, followed by a tapering off and decline. Most physics journals, they projected, would sell only 900 copies by the year 2000, only enough to fulfill "archival" purposes.[25] (I assume that this means only library subscribers by the year 2000.)

In a report at the same conference, Bowen stated that 12 of the 20 ACS journals had lost subscribers during the previous five years. "Further erosion of circulations will result unless successful sales campaigns can be waged to hold or expand the markets for the publications," he predicted.[26]

With the addition of *Sci Quest,* there are now 21 ACS journals. In 1981, 17 of the 21 journals lost subscribers, although most only lost a handful, and none are in danger. As it turns out, the ACS did not mount any major circulation campaigns in 1981. The low return rate from broad spectrum direct mail promotions makes it uneconomical to do so. Instead, spot campaigns appropriate for each journal are continued, to keep renewals high and to bring in enough new subscribers to replace cancellations. The American market is pretty well saturated for older ACS journals, Bowen feels, although he believes that a potential market exists overseas, particularly in underdeveloped countries. "But we don't know how to reach *those subscribers,*" he says.[27]

With the number of subscribers declining, the single greatest hope for publishers probably is to increase the subscription rate for their most solid customers—the libraries. The well-known fact that libraries are reluctant to cancel subscriptions to important journals no matter how high the price has led to the "institutional subscription rate." Individuals tend to drop their subscriptions at a certain point—$40 or $50 these days. Libraries stick it out at $500, $1000, $1500.

THE CONFLICT

This growth of the institutional subscription rate is a great bone of contention between publishers and librarians. Librarians feel that the institutional subscription rate is outrageous. Only a few years ago serial publishers offered libraries discounts, and most book publishers still do. Librarians catalog, index, bind, preserve and distribute journals. Without libraries, the documentation functions of journals would no longer work. Why, say the libraries, should they pay more?

Publishers are as convinced of their own special role, and the need for money to publish must override many other considerations. A publisher may take the attitude that no self-respecting physics library can get along without the American Institute of Physics (AIP) journals; therefore few libraries will cancel their subscriptions no matter how high the prices get. They can always ask the state legislature for more money because of the rise in acquisitions costs. Or libraries can cancel subscriptions to less significant journals in order to pay for the more important ones.

This attitude appears cynical to librarians and puts them on the horns of a dilemma. Herbert White sums up charges and countercharges over the institutional subscription rates:

> Librarians . . . can argue that they are in fact subsidizing unrealistically
> low individual subscriber prices. Publishers undoubtedly tend to counter by
> saying that price differentiation is necessary to protect what little remains of
> a personal subscription base. Without this, library prices would have to be set
> still higher. They also tend to argue that there is at least some suspicion that
> cancellation in individual subscriptions is accelerated by the availability to the
> library user of expanded interlibrary loan through networks, consortia and
> photocopying. . . . The charge that libraries are increasingly being asked to
> bear a larger share of the subscription price than in the past appears to be
> true. Librarians argue that they are being singled out because they are largely
> a captive market with little ability to make competitive decisions. Publishers
> respond that libraries are singled out to shoulder increased prices because,
> despite their poverty, they are still the most affluent group of subscribers
> available.[28]

But times have changed since 1976, when these attitudes were reported. Libraries are no longer affluent. Government funds are drying up, as libraries' costs are increasing. At the same time, as discussed above, publishers' costs are also increasing steadily.

GROWTH IN NUMBER OF JOURNALS

Given this rather desperate situation of libraries and publishers of journals, it comes as rather a shock to receive flyers announcing new journals. If the economics of publishing are so bad, librarians want to know, why are so many new ones being started? How can a new journal be important enough to buy? The librarian asks how the world got along without these journals for so many centuries, but now finds them to be essential to a well-stocked library. Yet, the faculty want them. This surprising encounter with a new scholarly journal is the way we experience the "explosion of serials" that the historians of science tell us is only a steady growth of three hundred years that continues in our time.

Fry and White concluded that new scholarly journals were being created at a rate of 3.9% a year; that is, 403 of 2459 journals studied were born during the time frame of the study (1969-73). On the other hand, they concluded that 2% ceased during that period, leaving a net growth in journals of 2%. They also found an increase in the number of pages published by most journals.[29]

A slower rate of growth is indicated by comparing the two most recent editions of *Ulrich's International Periodicals Directory,* although one must remember that *Ulrich's* lists many other periodicals besides scholarly journals. The 20th edition (1981) lists approximately 63,000 titles—1000 more than the 19th edition (1980).[30] More than 550 cessations are also listed. This would indicate a birth rate of 2.5% per year, and a net growth of 1.6% for the year 1980.

The King study concluded that 6335 scientific and technical journals were published in the United States in 1960, 8460 in 1974.[31] That amounts to a net increase of 2.2% a year. The number of journals per scientist consuming and contributing research remained quite steady, however.

The National Enquiry into Scholarly Communications, conducted in 1976-1978, found that journals in four disciplines in the humanities (classics, English and American literature, history and philosophy) grew more than twice as fast as the scientific journals covered by the King study. The growth rate for these fields was 114% in 15 years, or 7.6% a year.[32] This is especially interesting since Fry and White's study and the National Enquiry both found that journals in the humanities were in the most financial difficulty.

What can account for this growth even in hard times? The clue is the King study's figure for journal-per-scientist, which stayed even during the period of growth. The research literature grows as researchers grow, and hence, as research grows. White, in his summary of the Fry-White findings, says:

> Concern about this assumed rate of growth among librarians and others has been so great that suggestions have been made that libraries refuse to purchase newly published journals in order to force publishers to limit their output. It appears clear, however, that most new journals arise from needs of scholars and researchers to communicate the results of their research and the needs of others to learn about that research rather than from some preconceived notion by publishers that new journals in particular fields must be issued. . . . The net annual rate of growth . . . [of] 2% [is] a figure considered neither alarming nor abnormal when compared to growth in research, particularly academic research, during the same time period.[33]

The National Enquiry concluded that the ease of entry into publication is a good thing, but that failing journals should not be kept going artificially by subsidy and that further net growth of scholarly journals should be discouraged by "a continuing scrutiny of the usefulness and quality of existing journals as well as those that are proposed."[34] That scrutiny implies a cancellation of journals that do not measure up.

However, there is no indication that librarians, scholars and university administrators are organizing journal population control efforts. There are many cancellations, but they appear to be for the reasons Dr. Blackburn mentions: library budgets losing their purchasing power.

The new journals exacerbate problems already quite difficult. They add to budget stress; to overcrowding of library shelves; to strain on scholars to read, on secondary services to index and review, on the national and international library community to catalog and provide access to all useful literature, and on existing journals as competition for papers and subscribers. Is it enough to say that scholarship is growing and therefore scholarly media must grow? Shouldn't we ask, "Who publishes them and why, in such adverse times?" Shouldn't we ask, "Who writes for them? Who subscribes to them? Who reads them?"

WHO PUBLISHES THEM?

The Fry-White study found that commercial publishers started more new journals than other publishers (35.2% new journals in four years, or almost 9% a year). Society-published journals increased only 7.4% (1.8% a year), new university press journals grew only 5.8% (1.4% annually), but other not-for-profit publishers started 19% new titles (4.5% a year). The new journals appeared twice as fast in social science (20.6%) and pure science (20.1%) as they did in the humanities (12.8%) or the applied sciences and technology (10.5%).[35] (Apparently humanities as a whole is not growing as fast as the National Enquiry found classics, English and American literature, history and philosophy to be!)

In 1982 this author conducted a brief study of cataloging for new serials in recent issues of *New Serial Titles.* One thousand randomly selected entries from the May through November 1981 issues were studied. Cross references and entries describing foreign-language publications were disregarded. Of the 350 English-language entries, only 47 were descriptions of new journals. They were divided by subject as follows: 9 humanities; 13 social sciences (including business and law); 18 science (including medicine); and 7 technical. Publishers of these 47 journals were: 21 commercial; 13 societies; 8 university presses and departments; 3 self-published (publishers created apparently for the purpose of publishing these journals); and 2 government bodies.

As the commercial publishers are the most willing to gamble on a new journal, it is probable that they are most likely to kill one that no longer pays its own way. The overall balance of publishers then may be fairly steady.

WHO WRITES FOR THEM?

There is no problem for a conscientious and energetic editor to find publishable papers. As the National Enquiry report puts it, "Careers [are] at stake." Authors need outlets for their scholarly research. "Pressures to publish for professional advancement are strongly felt and generally accepted."[36]

This is not a recent phenomenon. Harold Wooster said in 1967:

> The young scientist learns, as part of the formal code of behavior of the scientist, that publication of the results of his research in a standard, authorized, refereed scientific journal is not merely right and proper, but a high duty and a behavior expected by his peers and employers. He learns informally that promotion comes about through visibility and that, at least up to a certain critical point in his career, visibility comes about through publication. He learns that there are "good" journals and others not so good, but that every manuscript can eventually find a home somewhere and that, for all the platitudes about refraining from unnecessary publication, this must apply to someone else—it is better to publish something in anything, even if only a government report, than not to publish at all.[37]

"Publish-or-perish" has a negative connotation, but it does not necessarily mean that bad scholarship is published. Scholars who might not otherwise compete for printed space in journals are driven to do research and to publish it. That can be very good for scholarship and society. However, it puts more pressure on the editors and journal referees to evaluate contributions and to publish only the original and creative papers.

Unfortunately, they sometimes are unable to do the job of weeding out articles which should not be published. One demonstration of this is the growth of what is called the "Least Publishable Unit" (LPU). Instead of writing one article about a research project, scientists—especially in biology and medicine—have recently tended to divide the data up into three or four articles, each only slightly different from the others, and to publish them in different journals. This leads to a fragmentation of data and makes the job of the researcher who is checking all pertinent references much harder. The only solution to this problem, says William J. Broad, is to expect editors and readers to do a more thorough job in evaluating papers.[38] It is probably not realistic to suppose editors will be able to reduce this practice significantly as long as grants and promotions are handed out to those who exhibit fat *curriculum vitae* with many publishing credits.

This sort of practice makes many librarians feel angry and worry a little less about cancelling subscriptions. More and more, they are studying journal usage and are cancelling the rarely read. Libraries may be very reluctant to subscribe to a new journal now. Editors of a new journal may attempt to find readers interested in a specialized field, but they will have a difficult time surviving without library subscriptions.

WHO READS THEM?

Who reads these new journals, and all the other scholarly journals being published so prolifically throughout the world? The National Enquiry found that "the average scholar scans seven journals, follows four or five regularly, and reads three to five articles a week." According to this report, these scholars spend 10 to 12 hours a week reading books and journals. More (40%) had increased the number of articles read in the past few years than had declined (20%). They tended to read their own subscription copies of journals, rather than a library copy, and scholars at larger institutions subscribed to more journals even though they had access to more journals in their libraries.[39]

A classic study of the reading habits of psychologists conducted in 1963 found also that American scholars did most of their reading in journals obtained by personal subscription. Most reading by foreign scholars was of library copies. Since all were reading the same 13 journals, 12 of which were published in the U.S., it suggests either that American scholars aren't as library-conscious as other scholars, or that all scholars tend to depend on the library for foreign subscriptions.[40] One also assumes that almost all psychological journals read by non-psychologists are library copies. (Of course, one cannot be certain that the findings would be the same if such a study were made today.)

The King study summarized its findings on the use of scientific articles in 1977: 5470 subscriptions per journal, 382,300 articles published, 244,000,000 uses, 638 uses per article, 2,092,600,000 article copies distributed, and .12 uses per article copy distributed.[41] This last figure is discouragingly low, considering the effort and expense mustered to produce scholarly literature in journal form.

Earlier reports by Elson and Dew (1955), Sorokin (1968), The American Psychological Association (APA) (1963) and Moore (1972) indicate that this situation is not a recent phenomenon. Elson and Dew concluded that an article in a specialized journal would be likely to interest only 10% of the specialists on that subject and an article in a general journal would interest only 2% of readers. Sorokin estimated that 15% of what is published is read by *nobody*. The APA discovered that half of the research reports in core journals are read or scanned within two months of publication, by fewer than 1% of subscribing psychologists; no report will be read by more than 7%, and even the most popular journal has a large group of articles looked at by fewer than 1%. Moore studied use of the *Journal of Organic Chemistry* and concluded that the average subscriber glanced at 17% of the papers in the typical issue and read half or more of only 4%.[42]

One reason for the low readership per article appears to be the expansion of scholarship itself, requiring more and more specialization by the scholars. Journals sent as part of a society membership must cover such a range of interests that fewer and fewer articles in each issue are likely to appeal to any particular scholar. This helps account for the viability of new specialized journals. The quality of papers may not be as high as those of the well-established general journals in the field, especially at first, but the special interest in a sub-sub-branch will appeal strongly to those researchers devoting their attentions to that specialty.

This phenomenon also accounts for a new development in scholarly publication: the bulletin (a newsletter-type news medium) that publishes original papers, especially short communications of work in progress. For example, Elsevier has successfully marketed one newsletter-type periodical for biochemists and has started others for neurobiologists and pharmacologists.[43]

Even librarians, who might be expected to be as conservative as anyone in accepting new publications, show considerable interest in new periodicals. Respondents to a survey sent out with the December 1980 issue of *Title Varies** listed 38 different serials as important reading for them. Each was asked to list his or her top five. Many publications (including *Title Varies*) were relatively new, and the fifth most read title, *Serials Librarian,* is a specialized, commercially published journal begun in 1976. In sixth place was another more general periodical, the *Journal of Academic Librarianship,* begun in 1975.

The many new publications contribute to the scattering of relevant papers in a discipline. S.C. Bradford discovered that in any large literature search for a given time period, a few key journals will provide a large number of the articles, but a very large number of journals will have one or two articles each.[44] Because of this scattering, a scholar attempting to keep up with a field can find perhaps half of the articles being published by reading four or five journals regularly. By subscribing to an SDI (Selective Dissemination of Information) service he can cover 80% or 90%, but it will be very difficult or impossible for him to manage 100% coverage.

The academic librarian also has a difficult time trying to cover subject fields. Worse, he must anticipate what faculty reading interests will be not only in the next five years, but in the next 100 years. According to the study of use of the Pittsburgh University Library by Allen Kent and his associates, librarians' guesses about the use of journals in the library are poor. Use follows the Bradford distribution. Of the six departmental libraries studied, "the percent of the titles in the collection used during the sampling period varies from under 10% to a high of 37%, depending on the library sampled. In general, a very small percentage of the collection accounted for the entire journal usage in the sampling period, and could be projected for the year as the titles used predominantly."[45] While almost all journals will

---

*A newsletter published by the author six times a year from 1973 to 1980. Its audience was primarily composed of serials librarians.

eventually be used, some will be used so infrequently that they probably could be cancelled with virtually no complaint from faculty and students.

NON-SCHOLARLY JOURNALS

This chapter has concentrated on scholarly journals because that is primarily where the "explosion" of serials comes from. That also tends to focus on the problems experienced by academic libraries. But all libraries experience much of the frustration of working with serials, and some of the non-scholarly journals can create the worst problems for libraries. Before leaving this chapter we will talk a bit about the very different problems, goals and economic considerations of these publishers.

The publisher of a scholarly journal requires very little capital to get started. His potential audience is easy to find. He has minimal expenses for artwork and design, and since his publication will have limited appeal to advertisers, he does not have to impress them with lavish displays or expensive color printing.

The reverse of this is usually (although not always) true for the publisher of a general interest, nationally distributed magazine. Millions of dollars are required to assemble an expert staff of editors, writers, artists, publicists and advertising account executives. Designs, page layouts and sample tables of contents must be made up months in advance in order to gain commitments from large advertisers. Expensive test marketing must be done in advance. A heavy investment in direct mail promotions and in impressive ads in other magazines must be made. Despite enormous expenditures, the chances of success are not good. For every *People* that made it, there are many *Shows* and *Vivas* that didn't.

The entrepreneurial publishers of this kind of magazine have a different purpose in publishing from that of the scholarly publisher. Communication of ideas (and making a profit) is the aim of one; documentation of scholarship the aim of the other. A big consumer magazine usually has an identifiable (and salable) "concept," which will help editors assemble articles, stories and other features that make it unique and indispensable to a large group of readers, and therefore attractive to major advertisers.[46]

Circulation for a major magazine will be handled by a highly automated "fulfillment service" company. These companies will be highly efficient in handling new subscriptions and address changes, but will require four to six weeks to make changes in subscription records. While responsive to claims for missing issues, they will not often be able to send another copy of the issue in question, since few copies are left over and they are discarded soon to avoid high warehousing costs and inventory taxes. Even though the fulfillment managers are suspicious and cynical about the high percentage of claims from the very small percentage of their subscriptions that go to libraries, they will try to be scrupulously fair and will extend the subscription by one issue for each issue claimed as missing.

Controlled Circulation Magazines

At the opposite end of the spectrum is the publisher of the "controlled circulation" magazine designed for a particular, small, carefully defined professional group—e.g., manufacturers of mining equipment, egg farmers, institutional cafeteria managers. These magazines will live on the advertising, since there are no subscribers. Those people on the "subscription" list qualify for free distribution by virtue of their occupation, and presumably by their ability to make purchasing decisions. The carefully audited mailing list represents a high quality group of potential buyers to the advertisers, who are willing to pay much more than the usual ad rates for a small circulation magazine.

Editors will gather together three or four articles for each monthly issue, emphasizing practical methods and how-we-do-it-good articles from leading practitioners. The editor and his staff of two or three writers will also scan a few pertinent scholarly journals and competitors for new developments in the field.

As production costs are low and income from the 30 or 40 pages of ads in each issue is relatively high, a fairly steady profit is possible, even though no one is likely to make a killing. Since most of these publications are owned by closely held family corporations, no one can be too sure just what the profit figures are. Libraries do not usually qualify for controlled circulation periodicals, but exceptions can be made—especially on the basis that students at a university are being trained to enter the field the periodical serves.

Special Interest Magazines

One interesting phenomenon in the United States in the past two decades has been the growth of "special interest" consumer magazines. They are popular, generally beautifully illustrated, and aimed at a very specific audience: readers interested in a sport (*Tennis, Golf Digest* and *Bodybuilding*), hobby (*Modern Railroading, Car and Driver, Backpacker*), locality (*Southern Living, New York, Texas Monthly*) social group (*Parents, Retirement Living*), science (*Psychology Today, Astronomy, Weatherwise*) or art form (*Ballet News, Art in America*). These magazines have tended to be very successful and their formulas have influenced popular magazine publishing a great deal.

MUTUAL NEED OF LIBRARIES AND PUBLISHERS

These are only a few of the variety of serial publications that libraries need to have in their collections. The difference in the aims of the publishers and the libraries creates problems for both. While most publishers respect and use libraries, they do not devote much consideration to needs of libraries before making decisions concerning their publications.

Libraries serve a diverse set of users who tend *not* to be specialists in the academic field served by a journal. (Specialists probably subscribe already and do not read the library copy.) The library thus provides an audience for the scholarly journal that is not in the mind of the author or the editor of the journal.

The same is true of other serial publications—the general magazine, the controlled circulation magazine, the special interest magazine and countless others ranging from the shoppers' guides to intellectual journals. Because its published indexes make articles easy to find, the library helps students read articles written for housewives, blasé young professionals, poultry farmers. The library lets local history buffs read 30-year-old garage sale ads. It provides important political and literary analyses to a large non-elite audience.

The publisher sends his serial out to the reader he has in mind right now. The librarian makes it permanently available to readers 100 years from now whose interest neither one of them can imagine. The publisher creates communication between the great minds of national and international society. If anyone else is ever to understand this conversation, to learn from it in future years, to become the great mind of another generation, we will need the library's ability to provide permanence to that fleeting communication. The copy on library shelves is permanently available to read. The index to it is also available only in the library. The existence of a library copy somewhere makes possible a reference or citation to an article written and published sometime. All these are possibilities expected by publishers, assumed by authors and relied upon by readers, but provided only by libraries.

The point here is not that libraries are valuable to society or more valuable than publishers. Without publishers there is no library. They form a partnership. The point is that libraries transform the objectives and accomplishments of publishers into something else which is valuable to publishers, but may not be anticipated by them. Since the immediate objectives of librarians and publishers differ, they clash, and they trade resentment and suspicion of each other.

CONCLUSION

"Economics" is known as the "Dismal Science." The economics of journal publication are dismal indeed. Costs to publishers keep rising and income possibilities are almost exhausted. Libraries are publishers' best hope for retrieving the additional revenue required, but library budgets have been stretched as far as possible. Additional increases to library subscription budgets in the amounts required are extremely unlikely. Therefore, hopes of finding new mechanisms for getting income from libraries in another form, such as copyright fees, appear to be doomed to disappointment. On the average, subscriptions to each scholarly journal tend to dwindle. This too puts more pressure on publishers to increase subscription rates to recoup their costs. These rates can only hasten the time when more libraries and individuals will be forced to cancel. A self-feeding cyclical mechanism is taking over, and no satisfactory end is in sight.

The enormous overall costs of the journal system are difficult to defend when widely disseminated journal articles average so few readings. All authorities agree that we cannot go on this way much longer. Some new system or combination of systems will soon be taking the place of the printing of journals and their placement in libraries for readers to find when and if they ever need them.

At present, cost may be the greatest strain serials put on libraries, but prices are not the only criticisms librarians have of publishers. Serials tend to create chaos by their unstandard, unpredictable behavior in frequency of publication, delayed publication, title changes, size changes, merges, splits, absorptions, suspensions and cessations. We will discuss these problems further in Chapter 3.

FOOTNOTES

1. Norman B. Brown and Jane Phillips, "Price Indexes for 1981, U.S. Periodicals and Serial Service," *Library Journal* 106 (July 1981): 1387-93.

2. University of Toronto annual report of the Chief Librarian 1975-76.

3. Association of Research Libraries, *ARL Statistics 1975-76 and 1979-80.* (It is likely that the discrepancy between the number of subscriptions cited in *ARL Statistics* and Mr. Blackburn's annual report is due to definitional problems.)

4. Association of Research Libraries, *ARL Statistics 1980-81.*

5. University of Toronto Libraries annual report 1979-80, p. 1.

6. R. DeGennaro, "Escalating Journal Prices: Time to Fight Back," *American Libraries* (February 1977): 72.

7. Ibid., pp. 69-74.

8. Ibid.

9. Ibid., pp. 69, 74.

10. American Chemical Society, *Proceedings* (1899): 15; (1901): 18; (1931): 21.

11. John K. Crum, "Sale of Reprints, Advertising, Single Issues, and Back Volumes," *Economics of Scientific Publications,* pp. 32-33.

12. American Chemical Society, "Annual Report 1981," *Chemical and Engineering News* 60 (April 12, 1982): 55.

13. Bernard M. Fry and Herbert S. White, *Economics and Interaction of the Publisher-Library Relationship in the Production and Use of Scholarly and Research Journals,* U.S. National Science Foundation Office of Science Information Service, 1975 (NTIS PB 249 108), pp. 251-292.

14. Marjorie Scal, "Page Charges; Who Should Pay for Primary Journal Publication?" *Economics of Scientific Publications,* p. 22.

15. *The Technical, Scientific and Medical Publishing Market, 1981-82* (White Plains, NY: Knowledge Industry Publications, Inc., 1982), p. 24.

16. P.M. Boffey, *Science* (1968): 884.

17. Scal, "Page Charges," pp. 22-25.

18. *Scholarly Communications—The Report of the National Enquiry* (Baltimore: Johns Hopkins University Press, 1979), p. 62.

19. Fritz Machlup, Kenneth W. Leeson and Associates, *Information Through the Printed Word,* vol. 2, *Journals* (New York: Praeger Publishers, 1978), Table 3.4.13, p. 137.

20. Crum, "Sale of Reprints," p. 32, and telephone interview with D.H. Michael Bowen, June 3, 1982.

21. Crum, "Sale of Reprints," p. 32.

22. Machlup, *Printed Word,* p. 137.

23. "Journal Costs Alarming Scholars," *Chronicle of Higher Education* 11 (November 17, 1975): 8.

24. Data based on information from *Information Please Almanac,* 1981, pp. 56, 63.

25. S. Chomet and E. Nejman, "Economics of the Physics Journal," *Journal of Research Communications Studies* 3 (1981): 194.

26. D.H. Michael Bowen, "The Economics of Scientific Journal Publishing," *Journal of Research Communication Studies,* 3 (1981): 172.

27. Bowen, telephone interview, June 3, 1982.

28. Herbert S. White, "Publishers, Libraries, and Costs of Journal Subscriptions in Times of Funding Retrenchment," *Library Quarterly* 46 (October 1976): 366. (Summary of the study carried out by the Indiana University Graduate Library School, funded by the National Science Foundation —often referred to as the Fry-White study.)

29. Fry and White, *Economics and Interaction,* pp. 172-181.

30. *Ulrich's International Periodicals Directory,* 20th ed. (New York: R.R. Bowker Co., 1981).

31. King Research, Inc. *Statistical Indicators of Scientific and Technical Communication (1960-1980),* (Rockville, MD: King Research, 1976) 2: 125.

32. *Scholarly Communications,* p. 41.

33. White, "Publishers, Libraries and Costs," p. 361.

34. *Scholarly Communications,* p. 42.

35. Fry and White, *Economics and Interaction,* pp. 173-176.

36. *Scholarly Communications,* pp. 2, 4.

37. Harold Wooster, "Books and Libraries in the Scientific Age," *Library Journal* 92 (July 1967): 2511-2515.

38. William J. Broad, "The Publishing Game: Getting More for Less," *Science* 211 (March 13, 1981): 1137-1139.

39. *Scholarly Communications,* pp. 43, 44.

40. Nancy K. Roderer, *Statistical Indicators of Scientific and Technical Communication Worldwide* (NTIS PB 283 439) (King Research, Inc., 1977), pp. 88-90.

41. David W. King, *The Journal in Scientific Communication: The Roles of Authors, Publishers, Librarians and Readers in a Vital System* (NTIS PB 296263) (King Research, Inc., 1979), pp. 258, 297.

42. F.W. Lancaster, *Toward Paperless Information Systems* (New York: Academic Press, 1978), p. 72.

43. Jack Meadows et al., "What is the Future for New Research Journals in the 1980's? A Discussion," *Journal of Research Communication Studies* 2 (November 1980): 141. (The ideas referred to here were expressed by Robert Campbell of Blackwell Scientific.)

44. S.C. Bradford, *Documentation* (London: Crosby Lockwood, 1948).

45. Allen Kent et al., *Use of Library Materials, The University of Pittsburgh Study* (New York: Marcel Dekker, Inc., 1979), pp. 68, 72.

46. See *Folio: The Magazine for Magazine Management,* May/June 1974 for several articles on starting a magazine.

3

Seven Principles of Library Serials Work

This chapter will consider the fundamental principles of library serials work and the problems they cause and solve. Along the way, it will offer some suggestions for improving operations for serials handling and control. Let's start with a story.

A CAUTIONARY TALE

Fledgling editor Josh McKinney (to make up a name) stands by proudly as his first issue goes through the addressograph, is labelled and bundled for mailing. He admires the look of this new publication, now totally his, no longer a stodgy red, blue and gold, as it had been under its former editor. The $50,000 for the design consultant was well-spent, he thinks. As the 15,000 chartreuse and green magazines finish their run, McKinney ruminates, "How clever of the designer to get rid of all the unnecessary clutter, the title, volume, number and all that other printing formerly on the cover. How cute of the artist to hide the new title, *High Honey Ways,* on the side of the pouch the honey bee is carrying."

Six days later, the university mail truck backs up to the loading deck and the driver wheels out two hampers with five sealed bags of U.S. mail for the library. A normal day. But this is also a unique day. Today's shipment has the first issue of the old periodical *Bees and Money,* now revamped, brightened and retitled.

As the mail is opened and sorted into alphabetical piles, *High Honey Ways* goes on the bottom. The mail clerk can find no title on it and doesn't know where to put it. Cathy, the Kardex clerk for the section S-Z, finds it on the bottom of her stack. She discovers the title on the table of contents page (p. 5) and passes it on to Ralph, clerk of the G-J's. Having no such title among his 5000 entries, he puts it on the sample shelf. A week later his supervisor tries cross references and periodicals directories, checks and rechecks the mailing label for a clue, and finding none, also assumes it to be a sample.

Another two weeks pass. Georgette, the serials librarian, looks through her shelf of accumulated problems, scans *High Honey Ways* and decides it has merits, and sends it to the bibliographer in charge of zoology.

Two months later, when she finds on the sample shelf another magazine with a four-color drawing of honey bees weaving a sampler with the words *High Honey Ways,* she recognizes it as something she has handled before. A thorough check of this issue still reveals no clues, so she writes the publisher asking why *High Honey Ways* is being received. It happens to go out in the same mail as a postcard completed by Hilary, the Kardex clerk for the A-F section, claiming the missing issues of *Bees and Money.*

The *High Honey Ways* subscription manager receives these messages in the same mail, and shows them to Josh McKinney, the editor. Josh is irritated that the library staff is so lazy and unintelligent and, worse, take up his time with their incompetence. He fails to visualize any of the processes that his two precious issues have undergone at the library. How could he? He wrote for and received letters from individual readers in their homes and apiaries. Even his fertile imagination cannot suggest to him the scene of a major library serials receiving section with 25,000 subscriptions, with eight full-time people sorting, identifying, recording and routing 1000 pieces of mail a day, two people paying for them, and one person ordering, one replacing, one binding, two creating a holdings list of them and five cataloging them.

CREATE A ROUTINE

The foregoing story illustrates several problems and principles of publishing and library acquisition of serials. It is a fabricated story, but it is based on several real incidents. In brief, it demonstrates that libraries deal with serials by creating a routine for handling them that minimizes decisions. That is the first great principle of library serials work.

When a serial falls outside of the channels of the routine it is *routed to someone who is capable of making a decision about it.* When publishers decide to change the routine they unwittingly create problems for libraries—and for themselves.

Serials Records

Long ago librarians began to take advantage of the primary characteristic of serials: a title shared by multiple copies and issues. Each issue varies from the others only by its number and can be positively and uniquely identified by that number. Therefore its receipt need be entered only by number on a master record for the title. That master record is not the catalog, but the acquisitions file.

A principle difference in the library's handling of serials and books is this: the catalog is *the* library record for obtaining access to a book; it is only a secondary record for serials, and a record of questionable use, at that. The computer may eventually change that difference and blur the distinction. For now, it is a fact in most libraries that the catalog records for serials are incomplete, out-of-date or altogether missing. This is because most libraries cannot afford to duplicate the central serials record, the complete file of current serials.

The library needs to keep a surprisingly large number of items of information about its serials. The information it has will make it capable of answering these and other questions:

1. Main entry?
2. Title? ISSN? CODEN?
3. Publisher?
4. Agent used by library?
5. Library order number?
6. How acquired: subscription, standing order, exchange, gift, other?
7. Number and date of issues received?
8. Date library received those issues?
9. Does order include an annual index and title page, and have they been received?
10. Where is serial routed?
11. Where is serial until it is bound?
12. Is it bound?
13. What volumes, years, issues, numbers or whatever does the library own and where are they?
14. Library call number, if any?
15. Who binds it?
16. What color binding does it receive?
17. What cloth is used by binder?
18. What is imprinted on spine?
19. What volumes have been bound?
20. Is a volume now at the binder?
21. If so, when was it sent?
22. What issues have been claimed?
23. When were they claimed?
24. Did the vendor respond?
25. What response did the vendor make?
26. Do we have a history of poor receipt of this publication?
27. What other publications do we receive from this publisher?
28. What other publications do we receive on this order number?
29. What other publications do we receive from this vendor, if different from the publisher?
30. What is publisher's address?
31. What previous addresses has the publisher had?
32. What is the vendor's address if the vendor is not the publisher?
33. Is claiming address different from payment address? If so, what is it?
34. What is publisher's deadline for honoring claims?
35. Have we paid for current year?
36. How much did we pay?
37. When did we pay?
38. How much were previous payments?
39. What are vendor's invoice numbers for these payments?
40. What is vendor's identification number for this title?
41. What is vendor's identification number for this library?
42. What were library's voucher numbers for its payments?
43. What other invoices were paid on that voucher?
44. What is frequency of publication?

45. What is subject of publication?
46. What publishers formerly published this title?
47. What are previous titles for this publication?
48. What publications were absorbed by this publication?
49. What publications merged with this publication?
50. What publication did this split from?
51. What publication split off from this?
52. What cross references are needed for this title?
53. How can this publication be distinguished from another with similar title and appearance?
54. What published indexes and abstracts cover this?
55. Where have reviews of this publication appeared?
56. Who requested this subscription?
57. Has this publication been reviewed for cancellation?
58. If so, what is priority for continuing its subscription?
59. Out of what budget was initial subscription ordered?
60. Out of what budget is continuing subscription paid?
61. Did library make a one-time order for back volumes associated with this subscription?
62. What is country of publication?
63. What is predominant language of publication?
64. Have replacement issues been ordered for this publication? When? From whom? At what price? etc.

Answers to further questions can be surmised from information accessible to library staff members or users:

65. On what date should library expect the next issue?
66. What issues should library expect to have received that it has not received?
67. When should a claim be sent?
68. Should library staff suspect that the subscription has not been renewed?
69. Should library have paid for renewal before now?
70. When should volume at bindery be expected back in library?
71. Should the reader expect issues to be published at irregular intervals?

All of these questions are relevant to the tasks of providing access to, insuring ease of receipt and handling of, and making decisions about future library actions concerning serials. But all this information creates an enormous record-keeping and information-access problem of its own!

Multiple Files

Most libraries keep these records in several files, not one. The file with most of the information is usually the central serials record—in many libraries known as the "Kardex" and in others the "Serials Visible File" for the brand name of the filing equipment. This is the acquisitions file with records of receipt, payment and claims.

Thirty or 40 years ago most American libraries had separate files for check-in and for standing orders of periodicals. Another file served the acquisition of gifts, perhaps another the exchanges, another the government serials. Any special acquisitions project, such as Farmington Plan*, was likely to have its own receipt file also. In the late 1940s and 1950s larger libraries began to centralize the records, literally getting them out of shoe boxes, catalog card trays and storage crates. They also copied some information from other permanent files, for instance the shelf list, serials holdings file, serials authority file and the card catalog. The creation of specialized staff followed. The central serials record became the core for new serials sections and serials departments created in many American libraries.

The primary function of the central serials record is to identify the publication being received by the library. An individual with 10 or 20 subscriptions has no trouble identifying any, no matter what changes in title or appearance occur. The library with 200 subscriptions also has no trouble identifying them, although it will need to keep careful records an individual would not need, e.g., for recording payments, receipt, special routing instructions, binding routines. A library receiving 25,000 serials keeps all those records, but first must identify the publication in order to match it with its record.

The library can easily identify 95% of the publications, despite foreign languages, covers full of extraneous and confusing information, covers differing from title pages, and complicated cataloging rules which might cause the entry to be far different from what might be expected. The other 5%, like *High Honey Ways,* can cause great difficulty. For this reason, ancillary files that serve to index and cross reference the central serials record will be kept.

The file itself will have cross references to remind the check-in clerk that *Denver Quarterly* (the title on its cover) is really the *University of Denver Quarterly* (title on the table of contents page). A file of former subscriptions and "ceased serials" will help identify the revived serial or the issue from a publisher who refuses to accept cancellation of a subscription. A file of subscription orders by order number may help explain why an unknown publication is coming to the library. A file of cataloging changes, including title changes, merges and splits, helps make connections between old and current subscriptions, or between the card catalog and the central serials record, if cataloging processing is slow to change records when a title changes. A file by vendor may also help identify a strange publication.

Decision Making

Once the publication is identified, the routine takes over. The record for a serial will instruct the check-in clerk in all details of its handling: how to mark it, where to send it, who to alert, what color to bind it, what call number to give it, whether to treat it as a sample, hold for invoice, return to publisher, send to an overseas exchange partner, or other task. Decisions about the publication need not be made again. They can be made once for the pioneer issue or volume. Ever after, succeeding issues can follow the trail blazed by the first piece, and no librarian or other staff member in authority need see it again.

---

*A cooperative arrangement among academic libraries for acquiring materials from underdeveloped countries.

Because libraries are organized to handle serials in this way, renewals of subscriptions are routine and automatic. On the other hand, cancellations are time-consuming decisions that come as exceptions to the routine. They usually require evaluation and study by several people, not just a librarian. No wonder that libraries have been so slow to cancel despite rising prices. But facing the fiscal crises they now face and the imminent possibility that no money will be left over after subscriptions and standing orders to pay for books, librarians are now finding the means to set staff to work on cancellation decisions.

"Create a routine for handling serials that minimizes decision." One product of this rule is the tendency by librarians to prefer complete holdings of a serial. Librarians should not be faulted for this tendency (as many critics have done). Very few if any librarians would choose to spend precious dollars on volumes which they are certain will never be used. In the absence of good predictions about use, however, librarians are right to fill in missing volumes in their runs of serials. A completed run eliminates an exception, and perhaps even the necessity for looking up holdings at all. ("*Time* magazine? Yes sir, we have it. You'll find it arranged alphabetically over there with the bound periodicals.")

Since the principle of serials work organization brings exceptions to staff members capable of decisions, librarians become more conscious of them. Thus, the missing volumes take on an outsize importance to the librarian. "Why is it the only volume of *Journal X* that people want is the volume we don't have?" (Because the other volumes they get for themselves and you never hear about them.) Librarians *can* be faulted for not seeking good use statistics to base their decisions on. (We'll say more about use studies and decision making later in this chapter.)

DEAL WITH EXCEPTIONS

The second principle of library serials work is: Exceptions must be recognized and routed to someone who can make a decision concerning them. Recognizing exceptions may be the hardest training job for the library serials department. Some people will never be able to do it reliably. Therefore, one of the ruling characteristics of a library acquisitions unit is that it will tend to hire intelligent, alert people, capable of high-quality, high-quantity production. They will typically have excellent language skills and the ability to handle detail.

These people will be expected to make hundreds of screening decisions a day, "Does this match? Is there anything unusual or curious about this?" Unfortunately, these are the people who will quickly become bored by a job with such small intellectual gratification. The serials department is crowded; other people need to get at the files; much of the work is drudgery. When a large group of talented, bright people work with frustrating problems in tight quarters, it is no wonder that serials departments are often personnel trouble spots.

It makes no sense in this context to divide the work in such a way that checkers check in, but a claims clerk claims the same titles. The checkers' experience in handling routine mail and their training to watch for exceptions suggest that checkers themselves should follow up on the problems with titles they receive. No one else can exercise the judgment they will have from seeing the patterns of receipt. Moreover, the responsibility for following up on problems will give them the incentive to keep clear, complete, reliable records.

It is probably healthy for the serials department to have higher-than-average personnel turnover. Most serials check-in clerks or checkers are at their best between their third and ninth months on the job. But the work is excellent training for other library jobs, and often these people earn higher-level problem-solving positions in the serials department or elsewhere in the library.

CREATE ACCESS

The third principle of library serials work is that access to serials is as important as access to books, but different and more difficult. A book is described in a catalog with entries by author, title and subjects, and perhaps by co-authors. Except for books that are collections of essays, the subject entries give generally useful access by subject to the contents of the book. The call number also locates the book by subject.

For most periodicals, the cataloging only describes the vehicle, not the contents. The *Journal of the History of Philosophy* can be described by title and by subject ("Philosophy-History-Periodicals") but that doesn't help anyone find the articles on Kant and Hobbes and Democritus. Neither is the call number particularly helpful, since very few people browse in bound scholarly journals. (They do browse constantly in current issues.) We'll say more about that later.

Since book cataloging is more useful, every serial that can be cataloged as a series of books should be. (In fact, AACR 2 requires this.) Monographs in series are cataloged as books with a series note to make the connection. When a series is cataloged as a serial but each volume is analyzed fully, the result is much the same.

The cardinal rule is to avoid the error of the "Cat Sep." blind alleys. The reader who wants volume 43 of a series should not find a dead end in the library's catalog that says, "Volumes in this series are cataloged separately. They may be found by author and title for each individual volume," without telling him what the author and title are so that he can look them up. The very least that can be done is for the central serials record to list the entries for such series to provide a way for the user to find what he needs. Baer's *Titles in Series* is a useful reference work that can help staff and readers get past this blind alley, but in my opinion it is irresponsible of a library to force its users to consult Baer to find entries for Cat Sep. series.

Scholars will often want a series to stay together on the shelf, instead of being split up by classification for each author and the subject of each volume. For instance the *Loeb Classical Library* and *Early Christian Writers* are often kept together. This works very well for the user because he can find individual volumes easily through the monographic cataloging for each volume or by browsing through the series on the shelf.

Periodicals, on the other hand, need accessible holdings records. This may be a card file similar to the shelf list with permanent records of volumes owned transferred from the central serials record as volumes are completed and bound. This file is the starting place for most libraries to automate serial records because it is a much simpler and cleaner file than the central serials record. A holdings list printed out from a computer file is portable, and can be used at faculty desks or at reference and technical service stations.

A high priority must also be placed on purchase of the indexes, abstracts, current contents services and annual reviews that cover the subjects served and the serials owned by the library. An index for publications not owned is still very useful. A serial with no available published index or not included in online data bases has very limited usefulness. Only browsers in current issues and those following up citations from other published articles will be able to benefit from these unindexed serials.[1]

Finally, under the subject of "access" we need to examine briefly the shelf arrangement of bound periodicals. Most large university libraries classify their periodicals and intershelve them with the books. This has the advantage of separating social sciences journals from humanities, science and art journals, but it does not make them more usable for readers who want books and articles on the same topic. Almost never will the classification of a journal be precise enough to place it adjacent to books on the same subject. Near, maybe, but not adjacent. That nearness may be useful enough. On the other hand, articles on a particular subject can appear in a number of journals widely separated on library shelves by classification of their "general" contents. Most scholars approach journals with a citation from an index or a footnote. A reader wanting an article on Lynd's *Middletown Revisited* can as easily go to a location for all bound periodicals as to the book shelves for general works in sociology.

The real reason libraries with many scholarly journals have classified them is to give them a definite location without ambiguity. Most smaller public and academic libraries, departmental libraries and special libraries shelve their bound periodicals alphabetically by title. An alphabetical arrangement is much more suitable in a smaller collection, where users know almost every journal received and are not confused by similarities in titles. Alphabetical arrangement by title has several advantages: it avoids the look-up step for the call number, it is easier to plan shelf space requirements in an all-periodical stack area, and it facilitates quicker reshelving of bound periodicals that have been used when they are physically separated from books.

The two points of view are ably discussed in two articles by Joseph C. Borden and Robert M. Pierson in 1965 and 1966.[2] Not much has changed since those articles to upset the nearly equal balance between the two methods of arrangement. They are so nearly equal in value that surely no large library with many bound periodicals would decide to change what it is now doing. Probably most smaller libraries and departmental collections within larger libraries alphabetize their bound periodicals. Most larger libraries and libraries with a wide-ranging general collection classify. Until another factor enters the situation, there is probably no strong reason to prefer one over the other. That new factor—collection security—may be entering the picture, and will be discussed later in this chapter.

RELATE BUDGET PLANNING TO SHARED DECISION MAKING

The fourth great principle of serials work is that the serials librarian is not in a good position to make all the decisions on which serials should be in the library. Budgeting and accounting systems should be set up to ensure that the people who share the decision making consider cost factors in their evaluation of what to keep and what to discard.

Predicting Price Increases

We know that the costs of serials will go up each year at least as much as the cost of living. The first problem is to predict the rate of increase—one, two or three years in advance —for budget planning. No one can do that reliably, so librarians must depend on the most recent experience they have had and project future trends from it.

The first place to turn is to the library's own records. Any well-run library should be able to refer to its total expenditures for serials for each of the past few years, although few libraries can say how many different titles they paid for. Those expenditures are a pretty good indicator of the trends of library expenditure, but they are not enough. Further analysis is needed. How much do the history serials cost and how much are the physics journals? Do the costs of journals for each field make sense in proportion to the strength of those fields in teaching and research for the university? It is costly to do the accounting necessary to answer questions like these, but it may be worth it. There are also other sources for the statistics that can help answer these questions.

Perhaps the best known analysis of serials prices is the annual article in the July *Library Journal* by Norman B. Brown and Jane Phillips, called "Price Indexes for [the year]; U.S. Periodicals and Serial Services." The mean price for institutional subscriptions for the latest year is compiled in 24 categories for periodicals, and 8 categories of "serial services." The serials chosen to represent each category are standard journals and periodicals most often subscribed to by libraries and cited by authors. Serial services are defined as "a periodical publication which revises, cumulates, abstracts, or indexes information in a specific field on a regular basis by means of new or replacement issues, pages, or cards, intended to provide information otherwise not readily available."[3] The lists of these publications to be indexed are compiled by a committee of the American Library Association, not the authors.

Each year this article calculates the mean increase in price for representative publications in each category and the cumulative increase in price from a base year or years. The base is calculated as 100 and subsequent years as a percentage of that. The 1981 article used three bases, 1967-69, 1977-79 and 1977, but in 1982 the article used the 1977 base only, to be in conformity with the calculation for the Consumer Price Index. The *Bowker Annual* reprints the Brown-Phillips tables each year in an article that also analyzes the price of books.[4]

The Brown-Phillips article has been supplemented each year since 1974 by an article begun by F.F. Clasquin and continued by Gerald R. Lowell of the F.W. Faxon Company. This article appears each October in *Serials Review* (before 1980 in *Library Journal*). Lowell uses the actual titles indexed in widely used indexes and abstracts (*Art Index, Biological Abstracts, Biological and Agricultural Index, Chemical Abstracts,* etc.). Therefore he includes publications not covered in Brown and Phillips' analysis: foreign publications and non-periodical serials. Lowell uses prices from the Faxon Company (one of the largest U.S. library subscription agents) computer file. The figures are also weighted to reflect the number of libraries (among Faxon's customers) that actually subscribe to each serial. Lowell also analyzes the average (mean) prices for serials paid by each type of library Faxon serves: colleges and universities, community colleges, hospitals, junior high and senior high schools, primary schools, public libraries, special libraries (government) and special libraries (business).[5]

Having the expenditure figures for your own library's serials and statistics that represent the costs of serials to other libraries, you still cannot predict exactly what serials will do next year. However, most libraries have lost ground to inflation in the past three, five or ten years and can still appeal for added funds on the familiar grounds that the library needs to catch up. As we all know, the tendency for legislatures, administrators and budgeting officers is to give no one all he asks for. Many libraries are suffering major budget cuts along with their parent institutions these days. Most librarians will have to deal with budgets that are smaller than hoped and planned for.

Now the budget for the library materials as a whole must be translated into budgets for books and serials, along with microforms, audiovisual materials, reprints, added copies, replacements and whatever other categories each library uses to plan and carry out a strategy of acquisitions. At this point many librarians have been lazy or inefficient. Since it is difficult to forecast the exact cost of serial renewals, some have merely treated serial renewals as a fixed cost and used one fund for serials and book purchases. Other librarians have budgeted an amount for serial renewals, but without any way to cancel large numbers of serials their budgets have been ineffective. After the serials have been paid for, what is left is available for books. The book fund has had to bail out the serial fund when the serial fund is inadequate for its purpose. With this system, libraries with major investments in serials have tended during the past 10 years to spend a larger proportion of funds for serials and a smaller proportion for books, as we noted in Chapter 2.

Allocating Renewals Funds

The administrative alternative is to produce an effective means of evaluating and cancelling serials. Every library, no matter how well used or small its journal collection is, will have some that are more valuable than others. If cuts need to be made, somehow, those less valuable serials must be identified and eliminated. The problem is to promote the all-out effort to find them.

One way to do so is to allocate renewals budgets to subject disciplines. In most libraries, faculty or library staff subject specialists recommend purchase of books and new serials. If they are made responsible for renewals for serials in their fields also, they may be quicker to recommend cancellation of less valuable serials. If serial renewals and book funds are both allocated by subject, the book funds for the subject will have to subsidize the serial fund that goes over. For some fields, the choice might soon be to cancel serials or to stop buying any books at all.

Care must be used with this method. Some fields are much more journal-dependent than others (for instance, chemistry), and their journals may be much more expensive. Allocations should take into account these differences and not force them to fit into Procrustes' bed. The librarian must also remember that to allocate the budget is to allocate the responsibility. Invariably, some will exercise it with great care and others in a haphazard, careless way. Some central control over nominations for cancellation should be maintained.

This can become a thorny, political problem when the library has forced allocations onto subject specialists. For instance, what if the *Journal of Biochemistry* is located in the chemistry library and allocated to the chemistry budget, but is used at least as often by botanists and zoologists as chemists? How do you tell the chairman of the chemistry department that he cannot cancel this journal at a savings of $140 to the chemistry budget, when you forced chemistry to accept the responsibility for deciding which journals chemists must give up? Most librarians who allocate serial renewal funds will want to retain an adequate undesignated fund for picking up such interdisciplinary serials. The problems of serials selection, usage and cancellation are analyzed more fully in the next section.

Budget Fluctuations

The librarian should also consider whether annual fluctuations in budgets should be reflected in annual cancellations and restarts in serials. If a lean year or two is typically followed by better budgets, it may be wiser in the long run to let book acquisitions fluctuate to reflect available money while serials, much more difficult and time-consuming to select and deselect, flow more smoothly and steadily into the collection. On the other hand, it is no longer easy to buy two- or three-year-old books. Ten years ago books stayed in print much longer than serials, but now they often go out of print in 12 months. Temporary fluctuations in library budgets may be much more costly to the library collection now than they used to be. It will still be preferable to keep serial subscriptions going at least one year with a poor budget, if for no other reason than that it takes time to do a thorough job of evaluation of subscriptions, too much time to respond to a sudden sharp budget cut.

SELECT USEFUL PUBLICATIONS

A fifth principle of library serials work is to select publications that will be used sometime by someone. Few librarians or library users would argue with the idea that a library's serials should be read; the trick is to predict *which ones* will be read. Librarians selecting a book for the collection have the same difficulty, but a mistake about a book usually doesn't cost as much. An unused book can sit quietly and inoffensively on its shelf gathering dust, bothering nobody. But an unused serial continues to come to the library, continues to occupy acquisition staff time, continues to cost subscription and binding money, and continues to occupy more and more shelf space.

How do librarians select serials that will be used in their libraries? In small public libraries and school libraries with 50 or 100 or 200 subscriptions, it is not too hard for library staff to observe what is picked up, asked for, talked about and left lying around. The periodical collection in these libraries will tend to follow the published indexes usually found there: *Readers' Guide* and *Abridged Readers' Guide to Periodical Literature.* There will be other periodicals, but the core of the collection will be basic, popular, indexed publications.

In larger public and academic libraries with larger collections and more extensive quarters, such supervision is not possible. These libraries will have many indexes and abstracts and probably online reference services. Unfortunately, even the most excellent indexes are no guarantee that the journals will be used.

Until the early 1970s, librarians were not that concerned with the questions "Are our serials being used?" or "Would some other serials be used more than some of the serials we have?" or "Can we justify continuing to subscribe to some of our journals if no one ever reads them?" Most libraries slowly let their periodicals collections grow as new publications were requested by patrons, students, staff and faculty. With few exceptions, old subscriptions were retained. Horror stories circulated of libraries that did not maintain steady subscriptions. "At X University, faculty had complete control of the library budget. When old faculty left and new ones came, the new teachers cancelled favorite journals of departed colleagues and subscribed to their own favorites. Years later X University library staff were still trying to fill in those missing volumes of standard journals cancelled so long ago by narrow-minded scholars who did not have the foresight to see the cost and frustration that would be caused by those gaps."

So libraries, with their tendency to get bigger and bigger, slowly enlarged their serials collections. They added likely-looking titles here, titles requested by faculty there, and cancelled almost nothing—until the 1970s, when increased costs forced a change.

Suddenly, libraries began sending communications to faculty members that read like this: "The library must find ways to reduce its costs, since our budget will not meet the expected inflation of subscription costs for the coming year. Please examine the attached list of journals that the Library Committee has identified as titles for possible cancellation. If all 132 of these subscriptions were cancelled, the library would save $10,000. Other lists of possible cancellations will be circulated later in the hope that at least $40,000 can be eliminated from our expected subscription costs next year. Please contact the serials librarian if your work will be seriously affected by the cancellation of any of these titles."[6]

First the expensive newsletters with questionable permanent value get the ax. Then duplicate subscriptions are painfully cancelled. A few journals of obviously less importance, and some of the foreign language journals, are cancelled. But then, after the investment of much time by staff, only a few thousand dollars are saved; not enough even to balance the increase in next year's subscription prices. The price increases are relentless, the budget unyielding. What can the library do now?

Usage Studies: the University of Pittsburgh

Many important studies were published by Trueswell,[7] Buckland,[8] Fussler and Simon,[9] and Morse[10] creating new tools to study the actual use of books and journals. Gore [11] and DeGennaro[12] contributed popularized versions that have had great impact. In library after library Trueswell showed a remarkably identical pattern of book use: 20% of the collection accounts for 80% of the use.[13] Then, in the late 1970s, a University of Pittsburgh study by Allen Kent and his associates electrified the library world. The University of Pittsburgh study showed that 40% of the books bought in one calendar year had not been used once in five years and predicted that use for these books in the future was low indeed.[14] Since this study, every librarian has had to ask questions about which of its publications are being used, whether others would be used more extensively, and whether purchase of unused materials is justified.

The Pittsburgh study used a different method to measure journal use than it did for books. Book use was computed directly from a machine-readable file of circulation transactions. Since journals didn't circulate, no file of information concerning their use existed. The investigators placed observers in six departmental libraries to watch people use journals and interview those people concerning their status and purpose.

Results generally showed low use. The study projected use of about 95% of all journals at least twice during the year, but only 60% were used 25 times or more and only 10% were used 100 times or more a year.[15] Costs averaged $4.45 per use.

The University of Pittsburgh study is an expensive type of study to do, and few libraries can afford to duplicate it. Moreover, its results would not necessarily be applicable at other university libraries. Librarians need to conduct studies of use at their own libraries as far as possible. Simple counts of bound volumes shelved or current issues asked for can help. A study of citations in student papers and theses can ascertain the importance of journals versus books as well as the relative importance of particular journals for various subject areas.[16] No use study will be perfect, but any local study will yield information which will help interpret and apply reports of other libraries.

The purpose of the authors of the University of Pittsburgh study was "to develop measures for determining the extent to which library materials (books/monographs and journals) are used, and the full cost of such use."[17] Considerable controversy exists about whether or not the study achieved its goal and reported reliable statistics (see Chapter 8). Nonetheless, the study is important because it alerts the library profession to the need for use studies and it does propose helpful procedures for librarians who need to make cancellation decisions.

Selection Decision Making

Three decisions are identified: 1) the decision to continue or discontinue a particular title, 2) the decision to begin or not to begin a subscription to a particular title and 3) the decision whether or not to weed particular volumes of a title.[18] To these may be added: 4) the decision whether or not to bind a particular title, 5) the decision whether or not to purchase the title in a microfiche or microfilm format, 6) the decision whether or not to acquire missing back volumes of a particular title, 7) the decision whether or not to store particular back volumes of a title.

The first three decisions can be based on knowledge from use studies: 1) Has the title been used since the library has had it? 2) Is the subject area of the journal proposed for subscription used heavily or not? 3) How heavily are older volumes of a title used?[19] The other four decisions are related to these questions, but are also dependent on the individual library's policy and facilities.

It might be feasible to place all journals in four categories: high use-low cost, high use-high cost, low use-low cost and low-use high cost. If this were done, it would be easy (according to the University of Pittsburgh study authors) to eliminate the low use-high cost titles, retain the high use-low cost ones, and study further the high use-high cost and low use-low cost titles. If judgments of value, either by faculty or the librarian, can also be attached to the journals, then the titles with high value but low use can be promoted to see if use increases. When costly, valuable, but underused journals stay underused, the difficult decision on retention will have to be made. Then the library will have to know whether it collects for present users only or for potential future users as well.

Perhaps the crux of the difficulty many librarians have with the University of Pittsburgh study is at this point. The study assumes and demonstrates that, on the average, use of older volumes drops precipitously. Therefore, a journal unread this year is likely never to be read. But librarians and scholars in the humanities, who are aware of many instances in which current use is not a good predictor of future use, are not comfortable with that assumption. The readership of the 1875 Sears catalog in 1880 is no predictor of the usefulness of that volume to scholars in the 20th century.

Even those who urge libraries to cancel unread journals would not disagree. They merely ask if every library needs to preserve the Sears catalog, or if copies in two or three libraries aren't sufficient. Even if someone wants to use a journal a week after it is cancelled and weeded, it is available through interlibrary loan or some other method of document retrieval. (Library cooperation in networks and resource sharing and their connection to collection development will be examined in Chapter 4.)

In discussing selection of serials, I have concentrated on the reverse: deselection. That is because I believe selection is not completed until a serial has been purchased and tested in the library. The librarian and faculty can read leaflets and ads and brochures about a serial proposed for subscription. They can read reviews and check such tools as core lists and *Journal Citation Reports.** The decision not to order may be made from these studies. The decision to order, however, should not be considered permanent until the serial publication has actually been acquired and has been available for use in the library for a year or two.

*A periodical published by the Institute for Scientific Information which charts citations in selected journals to published articles. It thus weighs the relative frequency of citations of various journals.

Its use should be carefully monitored and if not used, it should be a strong candidate for cancellation and weeding.

The objective of having serials that will be widely read should make librarians very cautious about cancelling duplicate subscriptions. Those are likely to be among the most used serials in the library and should not be automatically cancelled without careful consideration.

Another problem affecting the selection of a serial for the collection is its nature as a serial. When one selects a book he has the whole book, a complete entity whose usefulness can be predicted with some degree of accuracy. A serial is selected not only on the probability of the use that will be made of the issue or issues seen, but also on the probability that future issues will contain useful material. The difficulty is thus multiplied. Therefore the attitude of selectors should be hopeful, but skeptical. To make the final judgment, one usually will need several issues to judge quality of subject matter and tendencies toward improved quality, applicability or specificity.

As Davinson says, "In collecting and maintaining back files of periodicals, librarians are acknowledging, if only tacitly, that in order to preserve the significant they must tolerate much that is insignificant. To be able to forecast accurately which material is likely to be called upon in the future would be a great boon to the librarian and would release a great deal of storage space but it is difficult, probably impossible, to do this.[20]

ENSURE CURRENCY

The sixth great principle of library serials work is to speed the handling of serials to preserve one of their greatest advantages over books: their currency. A newsletter reporting newest developments in the stock market is worth very little to users who read it three months after publication. Therefore all library serials routines should be designed to expedite the movement of serials from mail room to public display. Some materials may even deserve hand carrying to save a few hours. *The New York Times,* for example, may be available at a local newsstand hours before the mailed copy is received. Its availability for users to read the day of publication is worth the expense and trouble of going after it.

Management decisions affecting early delivery of serials are crucial. If the Post Office could be induced to deliver mail at 7 a.m., it would be very advantageous for the library to pay premium wages for mail room or serials personnel to arrive early to sort it, allowing it to be checked in and routed throughout the library an hour or two earlier. Backlogs in checking in current subscriptions are intolerable and a sign of poor management.

Claiming, one of the library's more tedious activities, must also be done in a timely fashion. Publishers do not keep stocks of some serials very long. Serials librarians should know which publishers maintain back files and which do not. Faculty and staff have urgent needs for some serials as soon as they are published. Serials librarians should have those publications identified and should check often to make sure receipt is current. Various methods of claiming should be used for various situations, and the librarian should use the quickest means for solving receipt problems for the crucial serials. A long distance telephone call followed by a letter may be more expensive and require more staff time, but the cost and trouble are worthwhile if a few days can be saved.

One of the points of acrimony between publishers and librarians involves claims. Publishers wonder why such a disproportionate number of their complaints over delivery of issues comes from libraries. Publishers tend to mistrust librarians' honesty or competence. It seems to the publisher that librarians are either claiming issues received but lost or stolen in the library, or are claiming issues they received but failed to record properly.

Librarians should study causes of poor receipt carefully. I believe claims could be cut down drastically if *all* addresses used by publishers were carefully scrutinized and corrected. Some problems originate in mail handling within an institution—usually because of incomplete addresses. Other causes of claims that could be eliminated by libraries are subscriptions that are allowed to lapse and poor recording of date of receipt of issues. Another problem that could be eliminated is multiple-copy subscriptions with different expiration dates, which allow renewals to be credited to the wrong copy. The other main cause of claims libraries can do nothing to help: delayed and irregular date of publication.

PRESERVE VALUABLE MATERIALS

The seventh principle of library serials work is that materials of permanent value should be preserved. If a serial has permanent value, as much consideration should be given to its preservation as its acquisition. Forces that attack library materials include acid in the paper, organisms that live on paper and glue, readers who wear materials out, library processes that damage them, and vandals who steal and mutilate them.

Twentieth century books and serials are notorious for their acidic paper, which deteriorates in a few years. At least acid-free paper is used by some book publishers. No journal, to the author's knowledge, uses acid-free, permanent paper. Therefore the same measures needed to preserve books in the collection (deacidifying, low temperature and humidity) are applicable to serials, too.

Microfilm or fiche may be the easiest answer to preservation problems. While not cheap, it does save space and protect from theft and mutilation while it insures that the library copy will not disintegrate on the shelf.

Binding is a method of preservation that keeps issues together and protects them from damage on the shelf. Various kinds of binding are available, and more libraries should probably investigate economical, temporary binding for journals which need be preserved only a few years.

Providing security for the serials in library collections is a subject that has been neglected in recent years. More and more of our collections are subject to loss and mutilation. (Generally books are lost or marked up with pencil or pen underlining and marginalia. Serials are generally mutilated by the razoring or tearing out of articles or ads of particular interest.) Although there has been considerable discussion of theft of library materials, the phenomenon of serials mutilation and means of counteracting it have been the subject of few articles in the literature. Librarians know the problem is pervasive, however. In one recent study of periodical availability, 17% of citations looked for could not be found—9% because of articles torn out, and 8% because of issues missing.[21]

With a move toward resource sharing, each library will bear a larger responsibility to protect and preserve its collections, not only for its own users, but for the users of other libraries who will need them. This need to improve security may be the consideration that determines the argument between proponents of classified and alphabetical arrangement of periodical collections. A separate, alphabetized periodical collection could be maintained much more securely than periodicals interfiled with the books can.

The corollary to the preservation principle is that photocopiers save collections. People who are too rushed or lazy to take notes are tempted to take the article itself. An easily accessible, cheap photocopying machine provides them with an acceptable compromise. Publishers have often misunderstood librarians' insistence on the proximity of copiers to the collection. To publishers it looks like encouragement by librarians for everyone to make easy copies instead of subscribing themselves. Librarians are aware that a collection of periodicals that does not circulate and is not served by a copier will soon be a useless collection of lace.

In Chapter 4 we will have more to say about photocopying, as we discuss how libraries are sharing resources through networking and interlibrary loan.

FOOTNOTES

1. Cf. the most used and least used titles compared with index coverage in Lawrence J. Perk and Novelle Van Pulis, "Periodical Usage in an Education-Psychology Library," *College and Research Libraries* 38 (July 1977): 308.

2. Joseph C. Borden, "The Advantages of a Classified Periodicals Collection," *Library Resources and Technical Services* 9 (Winter 1965): 122-26; and Robert M. Pierson, "Where Shall We Shelve Bound Periodicals? Further Notes," *Library Resources and Technical Services* 10 (Summer 1966): 290-94.

3. Norman B. Brown and Jane Phillips, "Price Indexes for 1981, U.S. Periodicals and Serial Services," *Library Journal* 106 (July 1981): 1392.

4. Sally F. Williams, "Prices of U.S. and Foreign Published Materials," *Bowker Annual of Library and Book Trade Information,* 26th ed. (New York: R.R. Bowker Co., 1981), pp. 340-353.

5. Gerald R. Lowell, "Periodical Prices 1979-81 Update," *Serials Librarian* 5 (Spring 1981): 91-99.

6. Adapted from an article in *News and Views,* the newsletter from the *Health Sciences Library,* (University of North Carolina at Chapel Hill) 55 (April 1981): 1.

7. R.W. Trueswell, "Determining the Optimal Number of Volumes of a Library's Core Collection," *Libri,* 1966, 16(1): 49-60.

8. Michael K. Buckland, *Book Availability and the Library User* (New York: Pergamon Press, 1975).

9. H.H. Fussler and J.L. Simon, *Patterns in the Use of Books in Large Research Libraries,* (Chicago: University of Chicago, 1969), p. 7.

10. P.M. Morse, *Library Effectiveness: A Systems Approach* (Cambridge and London: MIT Press, 1968), pp. 84-110.

11. Daniel Gore, "Farewell to Alexandria: The Theory of the No-Growth, High-Performance Library," *Farewell to Alexandria, Solutions to Space, Growth, and Performance Problems of Libraries,* (Westport, CT: Greenwood Press, 1976), pp. 164-180.

12. Richard DeGennaro, "Austerity, Technology, and Resource Sharing: Research Libraries in the Future," *Library Journal* 100 (May 15, 1975): 917-923; "Copyright, Resource Sharing, and Hard Times: A View from the Field," *American Libraries* (September 1977): 430-35; and "Escalating Journal Prices: Time to Fight Back," op. cit.

13. For a summary of those studies see Richard DeGennaro, "Growing Libraries: Who Needs Them?" *Farewell to Alexandria, Solutions to Space, Growth, and Performance Problems of Libraries,* ed. Daniel Gore (Westport: CT: Greenwood Press, 1976), pp. 72-104.

14. Allen Kent et al., *Use of Library Materials,* the University of Pittsburgh study (New York: Marcel Dekker, 1979), pp. 9, 10.

15. Ibid., pp. 72, 73.

16. A study of thesis citations is reported in Harry M. King, "Subscriptions vs. Books in a Constant Dollar Budget," *College and Research Libraries* 39 (March 1978): 105-09.

17. Kent, *Use of Library Materials,* p. 1.

18. Ibid., p. 257.

19. Donald W. King in Allen Kent, et al., *Use of Library Materials,* p. 257.

20. D.E. Davinson, *The Periodicals Collection,* rev. and enl. ed. (London: A. Deutsch, 1978), p. 34.

21. Marjorie E. Murfin, "The Myth of Accessibility: Frustration and Failure in Retrieving Periodicals," *Journal of Academic Librarianship* 6 (March 1980): 16-19.

4

Networks and Interlibrary Loan

> Net-work n. 1. An openwork fabric or other structure in which rope, thread, wires, or other materials cross at regular intervals. 2. Anything resembling a net in concept or form, as by being dispersed in intersecting lines of communication: *espionage network; network of railways.* 3. A chain of interconnected radio or television broadcasting stations. 4. A group or system of electric components and connecting circuitry designed to function in a specific manner.*

Traditionally librarians have given highest priority to increasing their library collections. The biggest libraries have always been identified as the best and the most prestigious. The "serials explosion" and the economic crises of the 1970s have antiquated this attitude, however. No longer can any library be self-sufficient in its research collections. No longer can Harvard and Yale and New York Public and Illinois aspire to have *all* pertinent serials. Even the Library of Congress must make choices now, evaluating those serials worth acquisition, cataloging and storage.

Choices not to acquire materials of potential value to the library have been very difficult for librarians at major research libraries. Librarians at smaller university libraries (under one million volumes, let's say) and colleges are used to making this choice. To them, interlibrary loan is an important aspect of library service, and they expect their faculty and students to depend on a combination of local library resources and access to other libraries through such loans. At major research libraries, interlibrary loans may be considered a poor last resort—a necessary, but adjunct, service.

This chapter will discuss the importance of cooperative activities, particularly interlibrary loan, to libraries faced with the economic realities of the 1980s. It will also consider a related issue, photocopying, and the often conflicting attitudes of librarians and publishers to this form of resource sharing.

The American Heritage Dictionary of the English Language (New York: American Heritage Publishing Company, 1973).

COOPERATIVE PROJECTS: A BRIEF HISTORY

Library cooperation is not a new idea. When the American Library Association (ALA) was founded in 1876, one driving motive was the idea that together librarians could save time and effort (therefore money) by sharing their cataloging. There was no need for each library to have to catalog the same books over and over again. Cooperative cataloging was thus an early interest of the association.

Interlibrary Loans

Interlibrary loans had been discussed for many years, but became a reality in 1898 when one librarian, director of the University of California library, announced that his organization would lend materials to libraries that would return the favor. The practice spread rapidly. In 1907 the Library of Congress issued a policy governing interlibrary loans. In 1909 the Library of Congress made more than 1000 loans to 119 libraries. The ALA published a code governing interlibrary loans in 1916.

Why did interlibrary loans begin after so many years of library development without this service? The rapid growth of libraries and the cooperative movement resulting in and encouraged by the ALA created the atmosphere. Fast, cheap and reliable mail service made them feasible. Gordon Williams supposes that the most important factor leading to interlibrary loans was the rapid growth of new, small universities with ambitions to promote research and provide the same teaching excellence as their sister universities with a hundred years' head start and with rich, well-developed library resources to support their programs. Even the older libraries needed support, as curricula shifted to greater emphasis on graduate study, science and social science. The broad continent, with the wide dispersal of resources, made scholars' travel less practical, too. All these factors led to the development of interlibrary loans, which appeared to be the perfect supplementary, inexpensive program that helped everybody.[1]

In setting up interlibrary loan service, librarians were willing to help others from the richness of their collections, but they also expected the system to be a help to their own libraries. They assumed that the help given and received would be about equal. They worried about local users being inconvenienced if books were out of the library, but hoped that the inconvenience could be minimized. Interlibrary loans were given a cautious try, but the pioneers were ready to abandon the service immediately if local readers complained too much. Poor dreamers—how could they know that rarely would the local reader want a book that was out on loan to another library? The real problem with interlibrary loans turned out to be the overwhelming number of loan requests that the better libraries received. The patterns have become clear to us now. Larger, older, major libraries will receive five, ten, fifteen interlibrary loan requests for every one they send. We will say more about this later in this chapter.

Other Cooperative Efforts

There are other cooperative programs, notably in acquisitions and cataloging, that should be briefly mentioned here.

Cooperative acquisitions programs on a national scale were begun in the 1940s. The Co-operative Acquisitions Project for Wartime Publications in 1946 helped fill the gap American universities developed in their collections of European publications during World War II. This led to the development in 1948 of the Farmington Plan, which helped guarantee the acquisition and preservation in American libraries of publications of scholarly interest from dozens of countries. In 1956 a Foreign Newspaper Microfilm Project was initiated, and in 1959 the Latin American Cooperative Acquisitions Program began. Beginning in 1962, the PL-480 program used surplus U.S. funds in foreign countries to acquire books and serials from India, Pakistan, the United Arab Republic, Indonesia, Israel, Nepal, Sri Lanka, Yugoslavia and Poland and to deposit them in U.S. libraries.[2] Perhaps the last important such cooperative program was the formation in 1968 of the Center for Chinese Research Materials to acquire, imprint and distribute important Chinese scholarly materials not available otherwise in the U.S.[3]

All of these acquisitions efforts assumed the mechanism of interlibrary loans to make available to any researcher working through any library the resources acquired by one library.

Some projects in the 1960s formed libraries into regional and local associations to cooperate on acquisitions of expensive items; assign subject specialization; create union lists, catalogs and directories; and streamline interlibrary loans. Five Associated University Libraries (FAUL) in New York, Librarians of the Council of Independent Kentucky Colleges and Universities, the Middle Atlantic Research Libraries Information Network (MARLIN) and the North Dakota Network of Knowledge all had this pattern.

Other projects included state and regional cataloging and processing centers, and centers for the storage of little used materials that could cut costs and still make expensive research items useful to a larger clientele than a single college library. The Midwest Interlibrary Center (later to become the Center for Research Libraries), the Hampshire Interlibrary Center, and the Associated Colleges of the Midwest (ACM) Periodical Bank followed this pattern. A national program to save money on acquisitions and cataloging was also started in 1966, the National Program for Acquisitions and Cataloging (NPAC). This last program did not include interlibrary loans, but the product of its work, the *National Union Catalog,* made interlibrary loans work easier, and increased the pressure on libraries to borrow from other collections.

It is interesting that all the cooperative projects among libraries include interlibrary loans, or make interlibrary loans more crucial, or assume the existence of interlibrary loans. This continues to be true in the more recent development of the computer-aided library networks.

COMPUTERIZED LIBRARY NETWORKS

We could add to the definitions of "network" that we quoted at the opening of this chapter a fifth: "A group of libraries connected by a common program and one or more computers." The growth of such networks may be the most startling development in libraries in the past 100 years. It certainly has made changes in the way libraries do much of their business and allocate their resources. These national bibliographic networks have a considerable impact on interlibrary loans. At a time when more and more is being published and libraries can purchase less of what they want, we are creating a system of information that identifies better than ever what books and serials have been published and what libraries own them. What results can we expect: increased pressures for borrowing between libraries.

OCLC

The Columbia-Harvard-Yale medical library computer-based cooperative cataloging program led the way in 1963. This program died soon, but it set the stage for the spectacular success of the Ohio College Library Center, now called the Online Computer Library Center (OCLC). Fred Kilgour, associate director of the Yale University Library when he proposed the OCLC system in 1965, left Yale to become OCLC's director in 1967. OCLC was planned to help small colleges in Ohio be more efficient in cataloging by using the MARC machine-readable cataloging data produced by the Library of Congress.

OCLC went online in 1971. By 1972 libraries outside Ohio were clamoring for membership, and beginning with the Pittsburgh Regional Library Center, they were admitted. OCLC's success has been a real problem for it, though. The great numbers of libraries required an increase in the capacity of the system, changing the priorities in the system development. Many of the proposed services that were intended to be completed long ago were delayed for years, or indefinitely. The serials programs are still quite limited, acquisitions and circulation programs have not been implemented, and the cataloging data base still is without subject access. Nevertheless, the system has become a national and international institution. (The OCLC interlibrary loan system will be discussed later in this chapter.)

OCLC's success has had a great effect on other networks that began about the same time. NELINET, for instance, had ambitious plans to develop cooperative catalog card production and do other original programs. Despite the fact that many of these projects were well-conceived, NELINET had to drop them because of the cost of development, and because OCLC had become the standard system for all NELINET users. It was not feasible for the regional network to try to develop its own multi-library data base. Development costs were too high and OCLC was too well established. NELINET was reduced to the role of regional distributor of OCLC service. It has adapted to this role as other regional networks have, and has concentrated on training, feedback to OCLC, and development of related computer programs of service to regional members.

RLG/RLIN

However, OCLC has not swept all before it. Other bibliographical networks, established for local or regional needs, have developed into national networks. The Research Libraries Group (RLG) was originally started by Columbia, Harvard, Yale and the New York Public Library to establish a computer-based processing system suitable for the peculiar needs of major research libraries. In 1978, Stanford University became a member, and with Stanford came BALLOTS, the computer system developed at great expense by Stanford. BALLOTS was a flexible system with great promise for many applications and apparently superior access to a large bibliographic data base. It became the basis for the RLG's Research Library Information Network (RLIN). RLIN now has 37 member libraries in two categories of membership and a score or more "user" libraries.

WLN

The Washington Library Network (WLN) began in 1972 as a processing service for eight public libraries, one college library and the Washington State Library. Funding by the state legislature in 1976 strengthened the program; it has attracted 60 libraries in the Northwest and has been self-supporting since 1979.

UTLAS

A fourth network, the University of Toronto Library Automation System (UTLAS), was begun in the 1960s and was transformed into a service entity separate from the University of Toronto in 1971. It does not have "member" libraries, but simply sells services to any buyer on the basis of "connect time" or the products received. It provides a variety of services including online catalog data, offline products such as COM catalogs, and a sophisticated minicomputer inventory control system applicable to searching and circulation.

NETWORK COSTS

These four networks offer a bibliographic service to libraries and thus have come to be called "bibliographic utilities." They have different advantages and different problems, but their services have become essential for almost every academic and public library in the country and most of the larger special libraries. There are complaints about errors in the data bases and slow development of new and improved programs. The systems experience a lot of down time that causes member libraries frustration and expense while their cataloging staffs cannot use the system.

Miriam Drake estimated in 1979 that it cost the average library $20 to do original cataloging of a book, $8 to catalog it by adapting or reproducing printed cataloging data and $5 to catalog it from a shared catalog data base.[4] That makes networking sound like a great money saver, but one must remember that few if any librarians are actually cut from the staff when the typical library joins a network. At the University of North Carolina at Chapel Hill, the library paid about $110,000 in fees to OCLC (through SOLINET, the Southeastern Library Network) in 1980-81, a year in which it added 127,000 volumes. That fee was calculated on the basis of 44,000 "first time uses," 2000 reclass titles, and the production of 500,000 catalog cards, using nine terminals.

Joe Hewitt, associate university librarian for technical services at the University of North Carolina, points out that it is difficult to make a case for cost savings for libraries through membership in a bibliographic utility. Membership will help a library promote more efficient procedures which will provide a "reasonable opportunity to recover out-of-pocket expenses." Basically, he adds, networks don't save money. "What they do is to help the library create improved records with many implications for future library service we are just beginning to realize."[5]

CONSER

In 1970 the Library of Congress published its MARC (Machine Readable Cataloging) format for serials and began using this format in its cataloging. In 1973 this cataloging format first became available through the MARC distribution service. By that time the Library of Congress had created MARC records for 30,000 titles, not a small accomplishment. But it naturally cataloged *new* serials and made little headway in recataloging the 200,000-300,000 serials already existing in North American libraries. Librarians and scholars foresaw the unhappy prospect of handling basic periodicals and journals for years without being able to have access to the best cataloging for them.

A group of librarians and automation experts representing the Library of Congress, the Council on Library Resources (CLR), OCLC and others responded to this problem by the creation of CONSER (Conversion of Serials). CONSER was a cooperative project which allowed several libraries to aid the Library of Congress in recataloging the older serials. The data base of the Minnesota Union List of Serials (MULS) became a core list. Its records were not complete but they could be expanded into the full MARC format more easily than any other existing records. Several individual libraries contributed original cataloging, the OCLC network contributed its online facilities, and the costs of the program were largely underwritten by CLR. The Library of Congress and the National Library of Canada still maintained responsibility for "authenticating" the records and locking them in completed and permanent form in the data base. The initial phase of the project was completed in 1977, by which time 180,000 titles had been entered although most were not completed and authenticated.

CONSER has never been a perfect project. As of October 1981, a total of 348,739 titles were entered in the data base. Of these, 134,427 had been authenticated. But the changeable nature of serials has meant that even the authenticated and locked records become outdated and erroneous. A study in 1978 by Michael Roughton discovered that 23% of the serials records in the OCLC data base had errors, and of those, 29% had been authenticated. In other words, 6.7% of the total sample were incorrect but authenticated and locked. Most of these "authenticated" errors were due to changes in cataloging headings or rules or changes in the publications themselves. In addition, Roughton found that two-thirds of the entries were incomplete in one of the six basic fields for serials cataloging (often because contributing libraries could not assign an LC classification number). Of these, 32% (21.5% of the total sample) had been nonetheless authenticated (because without the original publication, the LC catalogers couldn't assign a number either).[6]

Not only does this mean that our best file of catalog records of serials used by thousands of libraries is far from perfect, but it means that every library that improves on these less-than-adequate records must do it alone, and no other library can benefit from any other library's labor. This defeats the whole idea of networking. We still have a long way to go in perfecting our national (and international) serials cataloging records.

ONLINE REFERENCE DATA BASES

There is a new chile pepper in the salad. A new service created by the computer has become indispensable in libraries: the computerized reference service searching online data bases. Most of these data bases are bibliographic, but some—for instance, the New York Times Information Bank—have actual textual matter.

The first data base came about as the by-product of a computer-constructed file. The National Library of Medicine began work on a broad index to medical literature in the 1950s. They called it "Medical Literature Analysis and Retrieval System," or MEDLARS. The computer was used to ease the problems of storing, updating, cumulating and printing the monthly and annual indexes. Whether anticipated by these indexers or not, the computer file became more important than the printed index it was creating. In 1965 it was made available to the libraries of the country, by shipping computer tapes for use at several computerized depository centers. In 1971 it was transformed into an interactive, online system.

Since then many other machine-readable data bases have been created. Such indexes as Science Citation Index were compiled by computer and the computer files themselves made available for online searching. Older indexes formerly compiled by hand, such as *Psychological Abstracts* and *Chemical Abstracts,* were converted to computer files and made available online. New compilations hardly dreamed of before were made possible by the computer and also became available online.

Martha E. Williams' *Computer-Readable Data Bases: A Directory and Data Sourcebook* listed 301 data bases in its 1976 edition, 528 in its 1979 edition and 773 in the 1982 edition.[7] Approximately 80% of these are online.

Local files compiled in special libraries, which are rich in a certain field or discipline, have been exploited for online searching. Massive government information files are also accessible online. Most of the data bases are provided to libraries by three commercial services: Lockheed Information Systems' DIALOG, System Development Corporation's (SDC) ORBIT, and Bibliographic Retrieval Service's STAIRS. In addition, the National Library of Medicine provides access to its own data bases, all based on the MEDLARS file.

Typically a student or professor wants to find recent references to a specialized subject and asks for an online search in the relevant data base or bases. After defining carefully the terms to use to get at the subject, the librarian or other intermediary runs the search and the resulting data are provided to the student as a bibliography. The larger and more comprehensive the data base, the more likely it will be that the student's own library will not own many of the publications. What next? Yes, of course, the interlibrary loan office!

Again, from another source, more of a load is being placed on the interlibrary loan system. The growth of reference service with online data bases can only lead to an increase in interlibrary loans—if librarians will only allow interlibrary loans to be completed.

THE INTERLIBRARY LOAN NON-SYSTEM

The scandal of 20th century librarianship is that every good and worthy library project assumes and depends on interlibrary loans as the fundamental, essential service, and at the same time we've insured that interlibrary loans do not work. Yes, we do successfully complete some interlibrary loans, but requests are a trickle compared to what we should have if the system were designed to succeed.

The interlibrary loan code governing these operations is designed not to open up interlibrary loans. The careful reader will note that it is full of restrictions limiting what can be borrowed and who can do the borrowing.

Interlibrary loans are limited to materials "for research and serious study," not for ordinary reading material.[8] The service "is an adjunct to, not a substitute for collection development in individual libraries." In other words, libraries are responsible for collecting materials they ought to have for the support of research and teaching in their own institutions or to meet the reading needs and interests of the public they serve.

If interlibrary loan transactions are denied for materials which are not intended for "research and serious study," then some borrowers are automatically excluded. In case the borrowing library is not strict enough, the code provides that it indicate on the request form the status of the borrowing individual. The lending library can then reject the loan on the grounds that the borrower does not meet the criteria for loans. The borrowing library should also "encourage library users to travel to other libraries for on-site access to material" needed extensively.[9] The borrowing library is also required to "screen all requests for loans and reject any that do not conform to this code." If any borrowing library consistently disregards the code, other libraries may refuse to lend to it.

The form requires careful bibliographical citation and verification. That is fair enough. The lending library should not have to spend time trying to find books and articles that do not exist or that have different titles or volume numbers from those cited. But many libraries do not have the means of verifying the more scholarly citations. Here again, this aspect of the form reveals that the interlibrary loan code in the United States is designed to protect the lending libraries from lending, a thrust directly opposite to the whole idea of our cooperative acquisitions and cataloging programs.

Even so, our great libraries have taken other measures to protect themselves. Interlibrary loan offices are kept understaffed purposely. If a library gave excellent service by sending books or serial photocopies a high percentage of the time within 24 hours of receiving a request, what would happen? It would undoubtedly receive a reputation and would within months be flooded with more requests than it could handle. To keep up with increased requests more staff would have to be hired, at increased costs and no benefit to the library.

A decent delay keeps things in balance. No library dares stand out as an excellent supplier of interlibrary loans. Originators of ILL requests will send them to many indifferent libraries, not inflict them all on one. Despite designed-in inefficiency, some libraries still receive too many work-causing requests and have had to institute fees for handling interlibrary loans. A $5 or $10 fee works wonders in keeping down the requests, and those that come anyway pay for themselves. It is a perfect solution for the large research libraries plagued by requests, but does not solve the national problem of supplying materials to those who need them.

What we have is a system that is not a system. It denies scholars and other readers the quick, easy access to books and serials that they need, it frustrates the library staff at smaller libraries who must wait and wait and apologize for delay that is not their fault, and it allows costs of service to pile up on the libraries which try to serve the general public, not on the libraries and readers who are served.

HOPEFUL SIGNS—AND PROBLEMS

There is hope. Change is in the air. A successful system in the United Kingdom and an efficient system in U.S. medical libraries may serve as models for study. Moreover, an OCLC computer application to interlibrary loans has cut out many of the delays inherent in the old mail system. These successes indicate that, if the ILL system suddenly grew efficient and quick, ILL transactions would skyrocket.

British Library Lending Division (BLLD)

The British created a new library unit for the express purpose of handling information needs of scientists not adequately served by existing libraries. The British Lending Library, under the brilliant and controversial leadership of Donald Urquhart, established a new standard for efficient interlibrary lending. Urquhart disdained to use traditional library methods and organization, but set up his collection as a "factory" which made available journals or photocopies of pages from journals for the least cost and in the least time. The British Lending Library—or British Library Lending Division (BLLD) as it is now organized—was established away from distractions of the city and was part of no existing major library. It started with its own subscriptions to scientific journals and, as it proved itself, broadened its mission to social science journals.

The BLLD has been phenomenally successful as an efficient provider of library materials. It received 41,000 requests in 1961, 2,104,000 in 1974. It filled a growing percentage of requests with photocopies over that period, from 7% to 40%. In 1963 it sent 13,307 photocopies in lieu of loans. Eleven years later, in 1974, it sent 893,801 photocopies, an increase of 6600%.[10] This rise is no doubt due to BLLD's exhaustive holdings and its standard of responding to loan requests within 24 hours.

One must certainly wonder what effect all this photocopying has had on publishers of serials. This is a major issue and a sore one for many publishers. We will come back to it for careful consideration, but the point here is that the potential demand for interlibrary loans is enormous, and if they could be provided efficiently, the actual demand would be unprecedented.

Medical Libraries

The Medical Library Assistance Act in 1965 strengthened U.S. medical libraries by setting up a national lending system in a hierarchical arrangement. Eleven regional libraries buttressed by the National Library of Medicine (NLM) acted as resources for all the medical literature any researcher or doctor in the country might want. NLM filled all requests with free photocopies—made possible by rapid improvement of copying machines. A definitive index, *Index Medicus,* identified the material that might be needed, and the system attempted to fill the need. This nationally planned logical system was eye-opening. It successfully filled a high percentage of requests quickly and, because of government funding, at little cost to the libraries or the users. Consequently, the volume of interlibrary loan traffic soon became tremendous.

Here we have another example of a government sponsored and subsidized ILL system. However, it is probably not the low cost to the user that has made it so popular and successful, although that has no doubt contributed. The efficiency and quickness of the NLM system is probably the reason for its high volume. Is an efficient ILL system possible without government subsidy? Our last example implies a positive answer.

OCLC Subsystem

The third example of the improvements possible in interlibrary loans came with the OCLC interlibrary loan subsystem which became operational in 1979. It simplifies interlibrary loans in two or three significant ways. It identifies a publication and gives a more complete and up-to-date listing of the libraries that own it than has ever been available before in printed union catalogs. Finally, it streamlines the ILL procedure by cutting response time and postal delays. In the old system, a loan request that could not be filled was returned to the requesting library by mail; a staff member would then have to decide where to send it next. The mail and handling delay adds eight to 14 days to the average loan request and at the end of that time the requestor is no nearer getting the item than he was when he turned in the request. With the OCLC system, the ILL request is received instantly in the terminal of the lending library. Even with positive identification of a location, the book might not be available; it could be lost, in circulation, on reserve, being repaired, for example. But the OCLC system automatically sends the ILL request on to a pre-selected library, so delay is minimal.

So far, the ILL subsystem has not been as helpful for serials as for books. As Ann Smith, interlibrary loans librarian at D.H. Hill Library, North Carolina State University, analyzed it, finding holdings statements for serials is more difficult in the OCLC data base because of the several steps required and duplicate records. The traditional typed ILL request form that depends on printed or COM (computer output on microform) serials holdings lists from nearby libraries still works best for her in most cases. "The OCLC system usually works very well for new serials, though," Smith says.[11] If the difficulties in locating serials records and holdings can be solved, the OCLC system should be as spectacularly successful for serials ILL transactions as it has been for books.

The idea was that the OCLC would reduce ILL business for the large libraries by making it much easier to identify copies available in the smaller libraries. However, the system apparently has worked so well that *all* loans have increased. The smaller libraries are furnishing more loans now, as expected, but the larger libraries have not been able to rest. The increased efficiency has apparently encouraged more loans, or to put it another way: the improved efficiency has reduced the discouragement of interlibrary loans.

NATIONAL PERIODICAL SYSTEM/CENTER

The inefficient interlibrary loan system has led to many proposals for reform. The burden felt by large libraries is as intolerable to them as the inordinate delay and red tape experienced by the smaller, borrowing libraries and their users. In contrast, the smooth, efficient working of the British Library Lending Division has invited ambitious plans for such a facility in the United States. In 1972 the National Commission on Libraries and Information

Science (NCLIS) proposed a National Periodical System.[12] The National Enquiry on Scholarly Communication recommended the establishment of a National Periodical Center. The Council on Library Resources drew up a specific proposal for a National Periodical Center (NPC) that called for a collection of 50,000 most-used journals, each with about 15 or 20 years of back files.[13] This center could be operated by the Library of Congress, but need not be. It would serve as a back-up to local and regional interlibrary loan consortia and networks. Requests it could not fill would be shunted on to the appropriate major library acting as the last resort. In that regard, the proposed center differs from the BLLD, which has created a collection of almost all scientific journals, and other serials of scholarly interest, in English and western languages.

The CLR proposal immediately engendered controversy. Some librarians felt that the proposed National Periodical Center only served the needs of research libraries.[14] Publishers, at first supportive, began to oppose the center as a threat to subscription income. The information industry opposed it as government-subsidized competition. Librarians argued over the concept of a small collection of most-used journals which would duplicate most existing collections versus the collection of little-used materials which could take the burden off many libraries to collect such materials.

The most devastating criticism, however, was contained in a report commissioned by NCLIS prepared by the A.D. Little Company. This report verified the great need for such a developed national periodical system but predicted that the proposed NPC would be less useful than projected. Opposition of serial publishers would probably mean many would not allow the NPC to acquire their journals, changing the nature of the collection from a solid set of most-used titles to a mixed bag with many important journals missing. Moreover, it would be out of date technologically. The proposal relied on postal service to deliver documents and printed copies and photocopies. According to the Little report, modern electronic means of storing and transmitting information should be integrated into any plans for such a major activity.[15] If they were not, according to the scenario envisioned by the Little report, the National Periodical Center would come back to Congress in four or five years asking for another $75 million in development money to convert to electronic storage and transmission.[16]

With the librarians in disarray and publishers and private information suppliers in opposition, Congress refused to act in 1980. The issue is still under study in 1982. If anything, support for the original concept based on the British Library Lending Division is probably dwindling, as the capabilities of the national data bases and bibliographic utilities develop. In 1982, a new effort to revive the National Periodical System with a National Periodical Center is being discussed by the Association of American Universities—Council on Library Resources Resource Sharing Task Force. Discussions are being undertaken with the Center for Research Libraries, with the object of creating a demonstration project of the feasibility of such a system.

EFFECTS ON PUBLISHERS

It perhaps goes without saying that publishers are worried by interlibrary loans and have fought hard against a truly efficient national system. Publishers, especially scholarly publishers, need all the income from libraries they can get. If there were an efficient interlibrary loan system, hundreds of libraries would cancel their subscriptions, leading to ruin for the publishers.

Williams and Wilkins vs. NLM

Williams and Wilkins, publishers, thought they saw exactly that danger in the National Library of Medicine interlibrary loan system. Every day thousands of requests came in and thousands of photocopies were sent out—some of them Williams and Wilkins books and journals. In 1968 they brought suit against NLM for copyright infringement.

This case was never satisfactorily resolved. Court of Claims Commissioner Davis agreed with Williams and Wilkins in 1972 that the National Library of Medicine was systematically photocopying and that this action was clearly deleterious to publishers. However, the Court of Claims reversed that ruling in 1973, holding that the library's actions amounted to the same as individual scholars making notes for themselves. The Supreme Court upheld the Court of Claims (barely) in a four-to-four vote, ending this particular battle, but really settling nothing.

Librarians and publishers rallied to take sides. The publishers claimed that the interlibrary loan service from NLM and other libraries depended on systematic copying which deprived publishers of sales and their rightful income. Librarians claimed that the interlibrary loan system operated under a long-established principle of ''fair use,'' which allows photocopying for an individual's use. The fact that the Supreme Court divided evenly on the case indicated that the issue would be heard from again.

After the preliminary ruling of Commissioner Davis in fall 1972, Williams and Wilkins expressly offered to sell to libraries the privilege of making photocopies. Journals which sold to individuals for $30 could be purchased by libraries with photocopying rights for $40. Librarians reacted furiously. Many refused to renew long-standing subscriptions rather than give any semblance of legality to Williams and Wilkins' right to sell what librarians were sure they already owned. Williams and Wilkins announced in December a change in their pricing. They agreed that the preliminary decision was not binding and therefore that libraries need not purchase the photocopying privilege. However, the revised subscription rate was the same for libraries as the previously announced rate with photocopying. Almost all librarians paid the new increased library rate without protest. It was not the first institutional subscription rate, but they were not so common then as they have become. It may be that the Williams and Wilkins case led many publishers to adopt the two-price system: one for individuals and another higher one for libraries.

ILL and Subscriptions

It would seem logical to assume that interlibrary loans hurt sales. Strangely enough, studies of the effects of interlibrary loans on subscriptions do not support that assumption. Most photocopies are from serials that are most widely used and most widely held by libraries. The expectation is that those would be the least requested, and we can only surmise that theft, volumes at the bindery or temporarily missing, or the need to replace articles ripped out of library copies may explain this finding. Whatever the answer, it appears that these ILLs are not at the expense of subscriptions.[17]

Librarians and individuals consider the availability of consortia or library copies when making a decision to subscribe or cancel, but it is a minor consideration, say the authors of another study. They found that the quality of a journal is by far the major consideration for both librarians and individuals.[18] Another study found that faculty were unwilling to cancel "essential" journals, but were slightly more willing to accept cancellation of journals of "moderate" value which were easily available on interlibrary loan.[19]

But, publishers say, there is a direct relationship between declining subscriptions and interlibrary loans. If interlibrary loans are efficient and easy, then a library has no incentive to subscribe. Librarians counter that, so far, interlibrary loans are not efficient, and publishers don't know what senior faculty are like if they think that faculty and librarians are in cahoots to cheat publishers of income by substituting interlibrary loans. Libraries, in fact, are spending every available dollar on serials, often much more than for books, and cancellations are the last alternative available when the money is exhausted. Interlibrary loans are cumbersome, and very expensive per use.

The National Commission on New Technological Uses of Copyrighted Works (CONTU) has developed guidelines that give specific criteria for libraries' adherence to the copyright law in photocopying for interlibrary loans. Essentially the CONTU guidelines require that a library cannot receive on interlibrary loan more than five photocopies of articles from the most recent five years of a periodical. Few libraries are having trouble complying. Librarians generally are happy to subscribe to any journal useful enough to be requested that often. For those few situations in which the subscription price is prohibitive, alternative methods of purchasing a reprint (from publisher, or ISI's OATS service, for instance) ease libraries' compliance problems.

Photocopying in the Library

There appears to be a widespread belief among publishers that the massive photocopying done in libraries is robbing them of reprint and subscription sales. The boom in copying and in interlibrary loan does correspond with declining sales, but many librarians (including this author) answer that appearances are deceiving. There is no connection, we say.

Millions of photocopies are made in libraries. Of that there can be no doubt. It is not librarians who are making them, however; it is the public who uses the libraries. Instead of laboriously hand copying an article from *Newsweek,* or the recipe from *Sunset,* the teenager and housewife make photocopies. Likewise, the scholar will copy hundreds of articles a year and file them away (unread). If there is no copier in the library, the teenager will not subscribe to *Newsweek* (although he might buy a current issue from the newsstand), the housewife will not subscribe to *Sunset,* and the scholar will not subscribe to the 25 journals in which he or she found pertinent articles. A few will write down a citation for future reference. Fewer will take notes for future reference. Fewer still will steal articles or journals from the library. Not many will do that, but enough to decimate the library collection. Copiers help preserve the library collection, and do not materially hurt publishers.

Publishers seem to believe that librarians are shoring up their collections by photocopying when they lack the money to buy the originals. It is possible that some librarians do this somewhere, but it is not very intelligent. To use photocopies, a library would have to create a reprint file. Ironically, they are more expensive for a library to handle, store, catalog, retrieve and circulate than the books and serials in their original format. The per-page cost in acquiring them is higher too. It would be a strange library budget that had unused supply funds and more staff than it could keep busy, but little money for books and periodicals. That would be the formula for a library to derive benefit from photocopying for its collections rather than buy the publications themselves.

Various studies have been made of the photocopying that is done in libraries. The on-looker would be surprised in an undergraduate library to see that people wait in lines to make massive stacks of photocopies of *fellow students' class notes.* Of course, the individual has the right to photocopy most printed materials for his or her own use anyway.

One study made by King Research, Inc. concluded that of the 38 million photocopies made in libraries only 500,000 would be subject to royalty payments under the new copyright law. Publishers did not believe this report, however, and set up the Copyright Clearance Center as a clearinghouse to receive and disperse royalty payments in exchange for permission to photocopy.

The center has collected $1,094,955 since its inception in 1978 and has distributed $223,036 in royalties to its 4549 member publishers (an average of about $47 per publisher).[20] Performance is improving but it is safe to say that this will not ever be a major source of new money, as was hoped. Study of copyright compliance will continue. King Research was contracted by the U.S. Copyright Office in January 1981 to conduct another study. This research is underway in libraries and publishing houses by questionnaire and interview.[21]

In 1978 Meredith Butler surveyed several libraries and their policy toward photocopying parts of books and serials for reserve reading. The 1976 Copyright Law says nothing about this library activity, and librarians have thus been required to interpret the law as it might be applied. Butler found a wide range of policies. Many libraries would place only one photocopy on reserve unless permission to copy had been received from the copyright holder. Others applied the guidelines for classroom use by analogy to assigned readings in the library. Those guidelines are much more generous.[22]

Despite variations in library policies and procedures under the new copyright law, librarians generally feel that they are standing up for libraries' rights, but are being fair to rights of publishers. Richard Chapin probably speaks best for librarians' middle course:

Libraries can, will, and should continue to make full use of Sections 107 and 108 of the copyright law and the guidelines for photocopying in libraries. To do less would be a disservice to scholarship and research. If we do not copy what we legally can, we will establish a pattern of restraint that might well shape future interpretations of the law. An active pursuit of legitimate photocopying, however, must be tempered by reasonableness. If we copy in an unrealistic manner, we might develop a body of case law that will restrict even what we now consider as legitimate.[23]

CONCLUSIONS

What is the effect of library networking and interlibrary loan on the libraries? They are able to provide better access to more materials for their users at less cost. To take advantage of the cost-saving benefit, however, librarians will have to cut acquisition of library materials for individual libraries, a painful reorientation of traditional goals for librarians.

The effect of networking on readers so far has been to create quicker, better indexing via the bibliographic search services, but to make them more dependent on interlibrary loans. That is a mixed blessing. Those working in medicine have had excellent service through the medical library system. The interlibrary loan subprogram of OCLC has improved efficiency, but long delays, unfilled requests and unrecompensed staff expense to some libraries are still unsolved problems in the majority of transactions in the North American ILL system.

Publishers and librarians still clash over ILL and photocopying. Librarians say that interlibrary loans do not cut publishers' incomes. Librarians still spend all they can on library materials, but declining budgets and increased prices have forced subscription cuts. Interlibrary borrowing is a second choice, not a means of freeing library money for higher staff salaries or boondoggles of some kind. In fact, if libraries *did* have to pay large amounts to publishers as photocopying royalties, the money would have to come from the budget for purchase of library materials. Some publishers might be better off, but at the expense of other publishers. Publishers remain unconvinced by this argument.

Networking and photocopying and copyright issues still divide librarians and publishers as no issues have in hundreds of years. A new strategy by publishers may obviate the problem by maintaining control of their publications in a new way—by publishing electronically. This and other new methods of publishing will be discussed in Chapter 6. First, however, we will consider another aspect of serials management: the use of automated systems.

FOOTNOTES

1. Gordon Williams, "Interlibrary Loan Service in the United States," *Essays on Information and Libraries* (London: Clive Bingley, 1975), p. 195.

2. William S. Dix, "The Public Law 480 Program and the National Program for Acquisitions and Cataloging of the Library of Congress," in Ligne des bibliothèques européens de recherche seminar 17-19 September 1973, *Acquisitions from the Third World* (London: Mansell, 1975), pp. 159-161.

3. David C. Weber, "A Century of Cooperative Programs Among Academic Libraries," *College and Research Libraries* 37 (1976): 209-10.

4. Miriam A. Drake, "The Economics of Library Networks," *Networks for Networkers* (New York: Neal-Schuman, 1980), pp. 240-241.

5. Interview with Joe Hewitt, associate university librarian for technical services, University of North Carolina, June 2, 1982.

6. Michael Roughton, "OCLC Serials Records: Errors, Omissions, and Dependability," *Journal of Academic Librarianship* 5 (January 1980): 316-21.

7. Martha E. Williams, *Computer-Readable Data Bases: A Directory and Data Sourcebook*, (White Plains, NY: Knowledge Industry Publications, Inc., 1982).

8. "National Interlibrary Loan Code, 1980," *American Library Directory, 1981* (New York: R.R. Bowker Co., 1981), p. 1699.

9. Ibid. It is only fair to mention, however, that the 1980 code works in tandem with a model code for library consortia which is slightly less forbidding. See "Model Interlibrary Loan Code for Regional, State, Local or other Special Groups of Libraries," *American Library Directory, 1981*, (New York: R.R. Bowker Co., 1981), pp. 1701-02.

10. Maurice B. Line and D.N. Wood, "The Effect of Large-Scale Photocopying Service on Journal Sales," *Journal of Documentation* 31 (December 1975): 234-35.

11. Telephone interview with Ann Smith, interlibrary loans librarian, D.H. Hill Library, North Carolina State University, May 28, 1982.

12. National Commission on Libraries and Information Science, Task Force on a National Periodicals System, *Effective Access to the Periodical Literature: A National Program,* (Washington, DC: NCLIS, 1972).

13. Council on Library Resources, Inc. *A National Periodicals Center Technical Development Plan,* (Washington, DC: CLR, 1978).

14. Donald J. Sager, "A National Periodicals Center: Too Limited a Goal," *American Libraries* 10 (September 1979): 465-66.

15. *A Comparative Evaluation of Alternative Systems for the Provision of Effective Access to Periodical Literature,* by Arthur D. Little, Co., (Washington, DC: National Commission on Libraries and Information Science, 1979): 6-7.

16. Ibid., pp. V-12, 13.

17. Williams, "Interlibrary Loan Service," pp. 202-03.

18. Herbert S. White, *The Impact of Periodical Availability on Individual and Library Subscription Placement and Cancellation,* (Washington, DC: NTIS, 1979), (PB80-111883), pp. 16-27.

19. Edward S. Warner, "Impact of Interlibrary Access to Periodicals on Subscription Continuation/Cancellation Decision Making," *Journal of American Society for Information Science* 32 (March 1981): 93-95.

20. David P. Waite and Virginia Riordan, "Copyright Clearance Center," *Bowker Annual of Library and Book Trade Information,* 27th ed (New York: R.R. Bowker Co., 1982), pp. 72-73.

21. "Copyright law's impact eyed by King Research," *Library Journal* 106 (January 1, 1981): 7-8.

22. Meredith Butler, "Copyright and Reserve Books—What Libraries are Doing," *College and Research Libraries News* 39 (May 1978): 125-29.

23. Richard E. Chapin, "A View from Michigan State University," *Journal of Academic Librarianship* 5 (July 1979): 128-29.

5

Serials Automation

Automation is a labor-saving, cost-cutting strategy that libraries have been adopting in various ways for years. Serials have been an obvious target for automation but relatively few successful applications have been achieved. As Dan Tonkeray has said, "Even with the assistance of outside funding, and the availability of third generation computer equipment in 1965, which offered cost effective online service, increased storage capacity, advanced operating systems, and time-sharing capability, most of those attempting serials automation projects failed. Those who attempted circulation systems succeeded."[1] To understand why that is, we must first discuss the weaknesses of the manual record keeping methods for serials.

MANUAL RECORD KEEPING PROCEDURES

Let us go back to the university library described in Chapter 3, and look over the shoulders of the serials staff as they handle mail and other tasks. Before we even get to the serials department area, we see one of the problems of serials. In opening and sorting the mail, the mail clerk routes all first class mail and sends the federal government depository shipment to documents, the periodicals to serials and the books to acquisitions receiving. All the blurbs, announcements, press releases, newsletters addressed to Occupant and other unidentified material go to serials. A half hour or so every day is wasted checking this material against the central serials record to make sure none of it is a legitimate invoice or renewal notice or an announcement for a series already on order. Since no one outside of the serials department is sure just what might be related to a serials order, the only safe thing to do is to let the serials staff see everything.

Check-in Operations

When the serials mail is opened, it is piled in alphabetical order. This is mandated by the alphabetical arrangement of the central serials record. But books in series do not stack in piles very well with quarterlies, weeklies that have been folded and rolled in mailers, and newspapers. Time is lost every day balancing piles of serials and picking up the ones that slide off and re-alphabetizing them.

At the central serials record file cabinets, each check-in clerk identifies the serials, finds the appropriate record, pencils in the number and date received in the appropriate box on the form, and marks the front cover of the journal issue or magazine with the correct routing information, or puts a streamer in a book with the same information. The clerk then takes the serials to the sorting table, where they are stamped with a library property stamp, counted and sorted onto the shelves representing the destinations of the serials. Misalphabetized serials and serials for which no entry can be found are passed on to another check-in clerk for further checking. If a publication has been passed around without anyone finding an entry, it is placed on the problem shelf. Duplicate issues are so marked and sent to the destination receiving the title.

Invoices are often inserted in books in a series received on standing order. Letters, forms or memos are often attached to serials received in response to a claim. Renewal notices are often enfolded with a periodical. These the check-in clerks separate from their attachments and route appropriately, the claim responses in the claim response box and the invoices and renewal notices in the invoice box.

While checking in at the file, the clerks are also observing and noting special information: a skipped issue to be claimed, duplicate issues consistently received which may indicate some other problem, a new address for a publisher, a change in publishers, maintenance or repair needed to an entry in the file (an old receipt form filled up, a wire bent, a hinge broken and needing to be replaced), or a title change. (The last will have to be documented for the serials catalogers and a cross reference made from new title to old entry until the change is official, when a new entry will be made and a cross reference will be needed from the old title.)

Claiming, Replacement Orders and Other Functions

While this activity is going on, the public and staff members of other departments of the library need to find information in the file. In this library, outsiders are prohibited from access to the serials file during the check-in time, but after 11 a.m., reference staff, bibliographers and acquisitions clerks intermingle with the check-in clerks and serials invoice clerks updating the file or getting information from it. In the afternoon the check-in clerks are largely occupied with claims—claim requests from departmental libraries, claims noted as needed during check-in, systematic scrutiny of the files for lapsed serials, and recording and sending to the appropriate destination in the library the responses of vendors to claims.

Since the university receives 25,000 serials actively, the file is too large to be used also for binding information. Those records are kept separately. The replacement clerk must handle his own records for one-time orders and must also make a note in the central serials record file that a replacement has been ordered. This alerts check-in clerks to give the strange out-of-sequence issue to him when it arrives, should the vendor ignore his request to send it with the special label addressed to him, or should the mail clerk neglect to read the mailing label carefully enough. The replacement clerk must also remove these replacement order notices from the central serials record file when the transaction is completed. At the same time, the order clerk is verifying the titles of publications that someone has requested as additions to the collection, and double-checking that the library does not already subscribe or receive them as a gift, or as a bonus on a membership.

The check-in clerks, the central serials record supervisor and assistant supervisor are pulled off their usual jobs in September when the renewal invoice arrives from the major domestic dealer. With everyone helping, it takes three weeks to record all the payments for each title on the invoice. Unfortunately, since the pricing information for many publishers for the next year has not yet been received, about a fifth of the titles on the invoice will have to have additional payments recorded later, when the dealer sends supplemental invoices.

THE PROBLEMS OF MANUAL FILES

This listing of the tasks being carried out in the serials acquisitions area gives some indication why automation of serials is difficult, and why automation of serials must succeed. The difficulty of getting information out of a large file which is accessed only alphabetically by title is immense. So much human intelligence and energy is wasted by such a set-up that any concerned human being must feel sorry for people caught in these jobs.

Size and Related Problems

Part of the problem with manual serial records for 25,000 subscriptions is the sheer physical size of the file. A small file—say 5000 subscriptions and standing orders—can be handled by one person checking and claiming and another person handling other acquisitions tasks. That size file has many advantages over one that must have four or seven or ten check-in clerks. Clerks need not pass notes back and forth so that the person receiving an item knows where it came from and what has already been done with it. Since one person sees all the publications, that person is much more likely to spot title changes or other irregularities.

Size is directly related to complexity. The larger file is more difficult to file in; thus a misfiling is more likely to occur and more likely to cause trouble. A look-up in the file is more subject to error and takes longer. The larger the file, the more difficulty check-in operations will have attaining good surveillance of receipt. In other words, libraries with many thousands of subscriptions and standing orders cannot claim their orders systematically as well as libraries with only a few thousand. We may assume that it is the rare library indeed that has 20,000 or more subscriptions and standing orders on manual records and that keeps up to date in its claiming.

The larger the file, the more difficulty the library has in getting all subscriptions renewed each year. The more subscriptions a library has, the more its address will be sold to advertisers for direct mail advertising programs and, therefore, the more junk mail the library staff will have to handle. The larger subscription list is more likely to have foreign language titles and publications by marginal publishers, who are less predictable and less professional in their production of serials and therefore cause more time-consuming problems.

It is efficient to bring together the many records of serials orders and receipts. Sheer size of the file causes physical problems, however. With a large file, the serials librarian faces the dilemma of whether to separate sections of the file so that check-in clerks can have their desks near their file work stations—thus causing more walking between file sections— or to keep the file together, and let the check-in clerks walk a distance from their desks where supplies and typewriters and personal effects are kept. A compact file is more difficult for other staff members to get at; when they are working at the file, they are more likely to disrupt other serials activities. A spread out file will cause more difficulty because a telephone will not be available at all check-in stations.

A large file with a large staff operates in more of a factory-like atmosphere. The library administration is more likely to want to "streamline" the operations of a large department, and most large libraries have understaffed serials acquisitions offices. They are staffed for the routine flow of materials, but not for the exceptions and problems and puzzles that need investigation. The accumulation of problems needing someone's attention is nearly universal in large libraries. They cause frustration and lead to morale problems. The larger serials staff is more likely to have staff turnover, which means that the department is more likely to be in the process of training new check-in clerks, or to be short a staff member during the interim between the old and new employees. More and more universities are using red tape in the hiring process as a means of delaying replacements and cutting salary expenses, and the large serials operation is more likely to be affected by this money-saving effort than the small one. (However, the small department will have a harder time trying to fill in for a missing staff member.)

Duplicate Records

There is a positive correlation between mistrust of one library department and another and the difficulty one has in getting access to the records kept in the other. Centralized serials records are far removed from departmental libraries and usually have restrictions on times they are available for consultation. It is well known that all departmental libraries keep their own check-in records, which of course duplicate the records of the central record. But they are necessary because the departmental library staff cannot use the central records to control the serials in the departmental library. Moreover, since the serials acquisitions unit is backlogged on claiming, the departmental library must initiate claim requests or no attention will be given to its lapsed subscriptions and missing issues. This is one of the severest limitations of the manual file. Each library spends thousands of staff hours a year duplicating records because of the inability of the main record to serve more than library technical services units.

Data Retrieval

The manual record has an even greater weakness, one that is becoming more crucial. The manual file cannot be manipulated to produce lists, statistics or other data for analysis. More and more we need to know what serials we get for each subject area and at what costs and in what languages. If the library is to examine its collection and cancel little-used titles, it needs to start with lists of likely candidates.

The reader may recall that in Chapter 3 we enumerated 64 items of information that the library kept in its files about each serial it received. If all 64 items are kept at our sample university library for all its 25,000 subscriptions and standing orders, it has 1.6 million units of information in those files. Despite all that wonderful information, when the director calls and asks for a list of American history journals costing more than $50, the serials staff will have to answer the question by checking the shelves of current journals in the American history section. They are helpless to retrieve such information out of their laboriously kept, information-rich central serials record, although some imperfect, but practical methods could be used. For instance, they could check the history section of *Ulrich's*, check prices in the current issues on the shelves in the American History section, if there is one, or call a vendor with computerized lists of titles retrievable by price and by subject. Imagine the problem when the new head of technical services wants to verify the running count of current periodicals (not serials) for the annual report to the U.S. Department of Education. The serials staff have no alternative but to drop their other work, go to the file and begin counting.

WHY NOT AUTOMATE?

If all this is true, why have libraries been so slow in automating serials acquisitions? For two reasons. The first is the nature of serials. Remember how much information is to be kept relating to each serial. Our sample library would not be able to create 1.6 million records with its present serials staff while they kept up with their regular duties. Once those records are created, those regular duties, particularly checking in the serials, still require an enormous amount of inputting. In fact, in a study conducted at Kent State University, it was discovered that it required almost twice as much time to check in serials on the OCLC system as it did on the old manual system. This would be a great disappointment to most librarians, especially after taking 18 months and 5000 staff hours to set up the computerized record system.[2]

Automation will solve the problem of retrieving information from the file and will partly solve the need to duplicate the central manual record. It will not solve the problem of junk mail received in the library or the problem of splitting up the mail among several check-in clerks so that no one person will see all the mail and have a chance to spot title changes. However, when one entry does not work for a problem journal, the check-in clerk does not have to pass it on to someone responsible for another part of the file. He can pursue it through the whole file without leaving the terminal.

Automation will solve the filing problems of manual files and will give much greater control over the claiming function. Automation will allow much better access to the library holdings records by the public, and will allow check-in clerks to work at their desks without interfering with access to the file by other staff members. But it cannot solve the problem of publishers sending their serials with inaccurate addresses. It cannot solve the problem of irregular serials, or regular serials unpredictably changing publication patterns or quietly dropping out of sight. It can't solve the problem of publishers changing the expiration date of a subscription instead of sending the missing issue. Nevertheless, automation can be a powerful tool which allows librarians to work at these communication problems with publishers and monitor more closely the behavior of their publications.

The second reason libraries have been dilatory in automating serials acquisitions is the cost of doing so. No library has been able to demonstrate that its automation project has saved money, although that usually is one of the primary goals. Time and again computerization projects have been able to provide marvelous improvement in service, and often new services not anticipated by the planners, but not a cost savings. Since libraries are looking desperately for cost-saving techniques, the inability of the computer experts to come up with any, despite many promises, has held up library serials automation.

It is difficult to estimate automation costs theoretically because so many local configurations and decisions about services wanted will affect them. Table 5.1 is an attempt to identify the kind of cost pattern that could be expected. Any library foolish enough to follow in the footsteps of Stanford, Northwestern or Virginia Polytechnic Institute and State University in creating from scratch a complete in-house integrated system could expect costs at or above the top scale shown in this table. Since those libraries and Online Computer Systems Co. sell their software, it is possible to use it as the basis of a standalone system for much less money. OCLC appears to be a moderately expensive alternative, with dedicated terminals, slow check-in and no help with claiming. The new Faxon and EBSCO systems appear to offer a relatively inexpensive opportunity to automate. The configuration that some feel offers the best service and cost-benefit ratio in the long run, a distributed network such as PHILSOM, uses a microcomputer and will tend to cost in the middle range. (These systems are discussed later in this chapter.)

SMALL-SCALE AUTOMATION PROJECTS

Many libraries have used automation in some way to produce a serials holdings list. In 1969 I was part of a team that created a printed serials holdings list at the University of Rhode Island from a computer print-out.

The old rotary file had become impossible to maintain, said the serials librarian. With the assistance of student keypunchers, we created a file of IBM cards representing the titles, volumes and years held. A six-digit number was given to each entry; this allowed us to space 20,000 entries with 50 numbers between each entry. The numbers maintained the file in alphabetical order. A card sorter at the computer center sorted and filed for us. A programmer at the center made the cards print out with the number suppressed and appropriate spacing on the page. The printout ran 360 pages. I pasted up four pages of printout into one 17x22-inch sheet 90 times, and a local printer with a good offset press produced 100 nicely bound 90-page 8½x11 holdings lists for about $2 a copy. The only capital investment by the library was for a wheeled IBM card storage file.

It never occurred to me until this writing that we were "Pioneers of Automation." We simply did an unsophisticated little job with first-generation computer technology and made our own decisions about how the data should read without any concern about stan-

Table 5.1 Costs of Automated Serials Check-in (Over Present Manual System)

Kinds of Costs	Basis for Figuring	Large Public and University Libraries (25,000 subscriptions)	Medium Public and Small University Libraries (10,000 subscriptions)	College, Special and Community College Libraries (2,000 subscriptions)	Small Public and School Libraries (500 subscriptions)
START UP COSTS					
Record Conversion		$25,000–$75,000 (at $1–$3 per title)	$10,000–$30,000 (at $1–$3 per title)	$1000–$3000 (at $.50–$1.50 per title)	$0–$500 (at $0–$1 per title)
Equipment Purchase[1]	$2500 per terminal; 1 terminal per 5000 subscriptions	$0–$50,000	$0–$50,000	$0–$10,000	$0–$10,000
Software/Design Modification	Computer staff man/years	$5,000–$500,000	$2000–$50,000	$2000–$50,000	$1000–$5000
Total		$30,000–$625,000	$12,000–$130,000	$3000–$63,000	$1000–$15,500
CONTINUING COSTS (per year)					
Staff	**A M[2]**				
	40 / 80	$13,500	$5400	$2000	—
	50 / 80	$8000	$3240	—	—
	40 / 60	$9000	$3600	—	—
	50 / 60	$5000	$2000	—	—
	60 / 60	—	—	—	—
	Claims (savings)	($0–$10,000)	($0–$5000)	—	—
Equipment	Maintenance or Lease	$10,000–$25,000	$4000–$10,000	$2000–$10,000	$2000–$5000
Software Maintenance		$2000–$20,000	$0–$10,000	$0–$10,000	$0–$5000
System User Fees		$0–$25,000	$0–$10,000	$0–$2000	$0–$1000
Estimated Range of Ongoing Costs[3]		$7000–$63,500	$3000–$25,000	$2000–$20,000	$2000–$6000

[1] $0 if equipment is leased rather than purchased.

[2] Check-in rates: 40 titles per hour automated/80 titles per hour manual, etc. Estimates vary widely.

[3] Not a total of cost elements, since no single system would consistently have the highest or lowest costs in each category.

Sources: Harry H. Kamens, "OCLC Serials Control Subsystem: A Case Study," *Serials Librarian* 3 (Fall 1978): 48, 54; James Fayollat, "On-line Serials Control at UCLA," in Clinic on Library Applications of Data Processing Applications of On-line Computers to Library Problems (Urbana: University of Illinois Graduate School of Library Science, 1972), pp. 70-72; Andrew D. Osborn, *Serial Publications, Their Place and Treatment in Libraries*, 3rd ed. (Chicago: American Library Association, 1980), pp. 194-205; F.W. Faxon Co., Inc. brochure on LINX system; EBSCO subscription services brochure on EBSCONET serials check-in system; author's estimates.

dards or compatibility with similar projects at other libraries. Most such projects have trouble in this area. When cooperative efforts begin, the local project has to be done over or adapted.

These homemade projects often have a second weakness: they are difficult or impossible to maintain and update. The creation of the first edition may go smoothly, but will the planners be able to build in continuity and the flexibility to allow for unforeseen problems? Will the project created by a team meld into a routine handled regularly by serials personnel?

BENCHMARKS OF SERIALS AUTOMATION

Many college and university libraries have successfully made that next step. If a library automates only one facet of serials, the natural first step is the holdings list. Most are probably printed out annually. Title changes, new subscriptions, cancelled subscriptions, added volumes and corrections are all added to the file kept on cards, magnetic tape or disc. For example, in 1969 the University of Alaska Library computerized its holdings list and created a computer file that is capable of printing out serials by subject.[3] The Iowa State University Library produced a book catalog in 1973, then upgraded it by changing it to a title entry catalog, giving complete bibliographical information, and creating an index volume that gives access to the list by corporate body, subject headings and title added entries. One of the beauties of this printed catalog is its use of the MARC format, unusual for the single-library holdings list.[4]

Both of those holdings lists are printed. Many libraries are now taking advantage of a cost-saving technology to produce holdings lists on microfiche. Working copies can be printed out by the computer, but the whole list can be updated at frequent intervals, say two or three months. Dozens of copies can be produced as COM catalogs, filmed directly from computer output without paper printout as an intervening step. This technique allows more complete updates and more copies to be run economically.

University of California at San Diego

The real problem that needs to be tackled is the check-in function. A good program for that function would also handle claiming and would produce the holdings list automatically, or would supersede the holdings list by making complete holdings accessible online.

The University of California at San Diego was one of the very earliest if not the first large library to automate serials check-in. The arrival card method of serials check-in was first invented in 1962 here. The system is built on the computer's ability to predict the volume and number of the next issue and to predict approximately when it will arrive in the library. As issues are checked in, the appropriate card is pulled from the arrival file. It goes into the deck updating the holdings. The cards left in the arrival file at the end of the month represent issues not received, for which claims need to be sent.

The arrival card system can also be programmed to produce a binding card when a volume is complete, daily arrival lists and lists of locations of its current issues for each departmental library.[5]

The library had some problems with this system that were caused by rapid growth, inadequate programming maintenance and inadequate documentation; these problems compounded by staff turnover at the computer center and at the library set the system back. These particular difficulties were correctable, but there were more troublesome problems inherent in the system design. The arrival card file became more cumbersome as it grew. The identification number did not keep it in order alphabetically, so cards had to be filed manually; this became a major task.

The worst problem was the limitation of the card itself. It only had room for 80 characters. To squeeze all the needed data on it, the call number was limited to 16 spaces and the title to 24. Since 24 spaces could not possibly suffice for many titles, mnemonic titles were invented. With 5000 entries, the mnemonic title worked wonderfully. With 10,000 it still was not a problem, but with 15,000 active serials, and the rapid growth which meant new mnemonics were constantly being created, the check-in clerks could not remember them. Filing and identification difficulties mounted. Moreover, the program was not flexible enough to handle unusually numbered series with parts and volumes, and other similar irregularities.[6]

In 1967 a new computer was installed at the San Diego campus and was made available for library administrative use. That seemed like a good time to devise a new system and to correct some of the problems of mnemonics. The new system used a printed list of expected issues rather than a card file. The list allowed for complete cataloged entries in a variable length field. It was easier and quicker to find the appropriate entry, and since arrivals were marked off the list, it was possible to identify new receipts immediately. The list method also allowed for decentralized check-in (although departmental library check-in lists had to be brought to the central serials department daily to update the master list). The list required a second step: the pulling of a transaction card from a file. This card, which is used to update the computer records for receipt of the issue, is filed in the transaction card file by a number that matches the number on the list.

At the same time the new system developed a more sophisticated method of predicting arrivals. Rather than identifying a pattern of receipt (weekly, bi-weekly, monthly, etc.), the new program depended on a 12-month calendar. In this way, the school-year-only journal or the bi-weekly except in July and August could be accommodated. With this refinement, nearly 80% of the titles could be predicted; this allows for automatic claiming, one of the more important functions of any good check-in system.[7]

Other libraries, for instance the San Francisco Public Library, have solved the arrival card problem by overprinting a complete entry on the card. Some errors can creep into the overprinting job if the cards and printer get out of synchronization. Even if this were to happen in only 1% of the jobs, it would be devastating if the computer were reading the cards that refer to one serial, the human check-in clerk reading others. This consideration led the University of California at San Diego to reject the San Francisco method.

System Development Corp.

Another variation of the list method was developed by the System Development Corp. (SDC) for its LIST (Library Information System Time-Sharing) check-in system. Cards must be punched to signify the arrival of the irregular serials, but the arrival of the predictable ones is assumed unless a card is punched to tell the computer otherwise. This idea requires accurate and current punching of cards to tell the computer than an issue it is expecting has not arrived. Most serials librarians will wince at this. Serials, even the most predictable ones, are never entirely dependable. Any system that assumes that all serials were received unless told otherwise is making itself too vulnerable to errors by the check-in clerk. The system does have the advantage of reducing the workload, since the issues that do arrive as expected would outnumber the ones that do not by 10 to 1.[8]

In January 1971 the University of California at Los Angeles Biomedical Library completed the conversion of a punched card system to an online one. With a computer facility devoted to the health sciences division and a system which allowed remote access to the central computer, the situation was perfect for experimentation with an online system. The new system was designed to improve on the card system by: 1) having the absolutely current records immediately available for consultation, 2) eliminating all card handling, 3) building in many points of retrieval with easy-to-understand routines so that relatively unsophisticated operators could run it, 4) eliminating inaccuracies common to card systems and 5) decreasing the need for many printed lists. The new system was also designed with the idea that other libraries would be able to adapt it to their needs.

The system reduces costs and improves morale by eliminating all the laborious card punching. Claiming is done with a computer-created file called "claim candidates." The claims clerk looks at each record for titles expected to be received and decides whether or not to send a claim. If a claim is to be made, the computer prints out the letter automatically. Since most of the work is done by the computer, the process is easy and fast.[9]

PHILSOM

The Biomedical Library at Washington University (St. Louis) began a program to automate serials records in 1963. The system was called PHILSOM (Periodical Holdings in Library, School of Medicine). It used an arrival card system with ingenious codes for telling the computer when to print cards for expected receipts. As this system matured, and with good programming and library support, it became more efficient. In 1968 it was redesigned with many modules, allowing other libraries to participate. By 1970 other medical libraries were joining, adding to the data base and changing PHILSOM into a network. The network operated in a batch mode, but was outstanding in its flexibility, allowing individual libraries to receive output in the form they wanted. System-wide programming changes were paid for by the PHILSOM network, but local changes were paid for by the local library requesting them.

Now PHILSOM, in its third generation, allows member libraries to input records online with data bases controlled locally. The network still operates with cards in the batch mode for some libraries (it is still cheaper) and provides the online libraries with batch mode printouts, such as analyses of costs, active and inactive data, and error lists, as well as one-time lists developed with a utility program. The network provides serials control only, but works with libraries in integrating serials data with automated circulation and cataloging systems.[10]

NOTIS

Northwestern University Library has an integrated data processing system for all technical services and circulation. This system, named NOTIS (Northwestern On-line Total Integrated System), was begun in the 1960s. The first version of NOTIS was never fully implemented, but the second version starting with circulation in January 1970, was successful. The serials check-in function was initially hampered by slow IBM 2740 typewriter communication terminals, but in 1974 these were replaced by more efficient CRTs. The serials module of NOTIS is outstanding in its ability to handle all functions related to serials in one record. Purchase orders, check-in, claims, catalog card production and invoice posting are all available to the staff member at any time. Likewise, the library reader can check for latest issues and back volumes and consult the circulation module to see whether the issue needed is charged out for binding, recataloging, repair or personal use in a study carrel.[11]

F.W. Faxon and EBSCO

In 1980 the serials dealer F.W. Faxon Co. offered its computer system as a serials control system for its customers. It allows online check-in on a shared-time basis to a central data base at the Faxon facility in Westwood, MA. The cataloging data base is based on the OCLC data base, but includes only those titles input by libraries using the Faxon system. In 1981 the serials dealer EBSCO made its system available to libraries. Like the Faxon system, it is an online interactive system but with a minicomputer at the local library acting as the central memory for the data base.

OCLC

The OCLC system has been working on its serials control program for almost 10 years. The first library to use the program, Ohio University's Vernon R. Alden Library, started using the program experimentally in 1976. In 1977 it was made available to other libraries, a few at a time, but it still is not a completely worked out system. (See Chapter 4.) The advantage of the OCLC set-up is that it is part of the network with the largest cataloging data base and has tremendous potential for integrating with serials work cataloging, interlibrary loan and other routines.

With the OCLC serials check-in system, many libraries are stepping off into the deep water. Until this network development, comparatively few libraries had tried serials automation, despite the great need and the tremendous development in computer hardware and software.

National Library of Medicine

As our final benchmark in the automation of serials, we can note two announcements made in early 1981. In January the Lister Hill National Center for Biomedical Communications of the National Library of Medicine announced the availability of its integrated library system through the National Technical Information Service. This system has a master bibliographic file, a circulation system and a serials check-in program. The master bibliographic file can use data from other bibliographic source tapes such as the Library of

Congress, OCLC, Blackwell North America and other similar sources. The serials check-in program allows for the local creation of bar codes directly from the master data file. The terminal has an inexpensive printer attached to it, allowing for the automatic production of routing slips during the check-in routine. The check-in updates the master data file immediately. The system will grow to allow for interlibrary loans, reserve and other functions.[12]

In a later announcement, the Online Computer Systems Co. announced that it was marketing the first automated library system for a minimum of $50,000.[13] Called Online, it is the same integrated library system developed by the National Library of Medicine. Online, besides furnishing the NTIS documentation of the system, offers a wide range of services, including library systems analysis and design, custom software and modifications, hardware acquisition for its customers, and user training. Online's services also include an optional interface with the OCLC terminal to enable the library to add to the system's master bibliographic file while cataloging on the OCLC system.

CURRENT STATE OF THE ART

The automation of serials has been slow and difficult. Problems in handling enormous amounts of data and incessant change in the data made the early computer systems, which were dependent on punched cards, cumbersome, labor-intensive and prone to error. Nevertheless, a few pioneer libraries with persistence and intelligent programming were able to devise good systems that are still useful. Punched card systems are used by many libraries to create holdings lists, and are successful as check-in applications in libraries with less than 5000 serial titles. However, computer technology and library system design have largely made card systems obsolete.

Online, interactive systems with CRT terminals for input and communication with the computer are now cost effective compared to punched card systems. The online systems appear to cut staff costs by reducing card punching and handling, but overall costs may not be reduced because they require more sophisticated and expensive staff. The improvement in control of the system is tremendous, however, and the online systems have the potential for improving productivity of serials staff in the area of claims. If improved claiming cuts a library's need to purchase replacement issues on the expensive out of print market, it could have important financial benefits to the library.

The perfect system has still not appeared, although almost all of the features of that system are now in use. Those features are: networking, a national data base, national (and international) standards, integration of functions and distributed processing.

The pioneer libraries deserve our praise and admiration, but not our emulation. Development costs for automated library systems have been extremely high. No library can afford to go it alone anymore. The existence of a national cataloging data base is acting as a magnet for all other cooperative library activities. Home-grown systems not only cost too much, but almost surely will not be compatible with national network development and will either have to be abandoned one day, or go through the additional expense of adaptation and modification.

The national data base for serials is growing, but is still inadequate. The OCLC data base now contains more than 250,000 serials records, but too many of them have not been authenticated by the Library of Congress. The use of such a national data base eliminates the costly process of original description during data input at an individual library.

The national data base is not possible without a national standard for the elements in the entry of that data. With MARC II we have that necessary standard. Any library that decides to create systems with shortened or below-standard entries is sure to regret the decision before long. Some functions, such as circulation, do not need the full data, but their records should be compatible with the full cataloging file. The cost of converting a substandard file of data later will be painful. The cost of not converting it may limit participation in library networks, which may be even more painful.[14]

Powerful standalone serials systems are becoming available at more and more reasonable prices as computer technology and software development continue their impressive advances. But no serials system will remain satisfactory if it is not part of an integrated automated library system, with cataloging, interlibrary loan, binding, reference, indexing, circulation and financial controls.

The hookup to a national data base by dedicated line will eventually prove to be too expensive a method for handling certain locally controlled functions, particularly circulation, accounting and serials check-in. The technological advances in computers allow the creation of new systems, such as the PHILSOM online system, and one being contemplated by EBSCO which would use a local microcomputer for online check-in and which would access the national data base only for the creation and searching of cataloging data, interlibrary loans and other network-wide functions.

All these features exist in serials control systems now in operation, but no super-system uses and integrates them all. Unfortunately, or fortunately, by the time (one or two years) such a system is created, it will be obsolete. New hardware and the system capabilities they make possible are being announced with such rapidity, that any system designed to use the latest computer and telecommunications configuration will, by the time it is ready, have failed to anticipate new, more powerful and cheaper components. New possibilities that appear to be almost upon us are: the integration of video disc memory, ink jet or electrostatic printing and improved resolution for CRTs.

DO'S AND DON'TS

The literature on serials automation contains many rules or aphorisms that deserve to be repeated. Priscilla Mayden, who directed the Spencer S. Eccles Health Sciences Library at the University of Utah during its conversion to an automated system, contributes five excellent rules learned the hard way:

1. Involve the whole staff in planning. The administrator may think that it will take too much time to involve public services librarians and that they may not be as concerned as technical services staff in the automation of technical services functions. But public services

staff are concerned. They have to interpret the records to the public. Moreover, those who are left out of the planning for a major library development are likely to have negative attitudes toward it.

2. Maintain manual records during the switchover period. It is expensive to do double work, but that is the necessary cost of conversion. It will cost much more if the new system fails and the library is left without any usable records.

3. The library administrator in charge must know the details and have a working knowledge of the automation system in order to substitute in an emergency, and to be able to make wise plans and realistic management decisions.

4. Train a back-up for everybody. What if one person leaves and another person who is given more of the load to carry gets disgusted and quits?

5. Never start an automation project with a budget barely adequate to cover the plan if everything runs smoothly. It won't. The plan must be detailed and the budget must cover contingencies.[15]

Richard DeGennaro, always quotable, adds more rules for us:

6. Don't assume that automation will save money. "When we first started to use computers in libraries 15 years ago, we thought we would save money, but we soon learned that there would be no net savings from automation." The reasons for this are the high development costs, the high capital investments and the surprises: the need for more highly trained and therefore expensive staff, and the computer's requirement that the quality of its records have a higher standard of accuracy than manual records need. Moreover, the computer makes new services possible, but these new services are more expensive. For instance, computer searching of data bases is a great advance over searching printed indexes, but it is more costly to the library in staff time.

7. We cannot settle for half-automation, half-manual records. "The single most important thing libraries can do to improve management, hasten automation, and reduce the expense and difficulties of maintaining parallel manual and machine systems is to convert their retrospective catalogs to machine-readable form and consolidate all their bibliographic records into a single integrated system. Libraries cannot take full advantage of automation until they can implement integrated systems, and they cannot have integrated systems while a substantial portion of their records is on cards in traditional catalogs."[16]

To these we may add the testimony of many:

8. Most computer personnel do not understand libraries. Therefore, for library automation to work, librarians must learn enough about automation to oversee the creation of the system.

9. The library will have lowest priority for computer time. It will take much convincing that books circulate every day and serials are received every day, and the library cannot wait for a week or two for its job to be attended to.

10. Service is the ultimate test of any system. It is a failure if it only makes life easier for the librarian, but does not aid the reader to use the library more effectively.

PROBLEMS SOLVED AND PROBLEMS REMAINING

National and international standards are paving the way for effective automation. The International Serials Data System with its ISSN is beginning to have a great effect in controlling serials. Most online systems now use the ISSN as a point of retrieval. Most major U.S. publishers have adopted the ISSN.

The CODEN system, using five letters and a check digit instead of numbers, still has many backers among publishers of scientific journals. The advantage of CODEN is that the alphabet allows more combinations with fewer characters, and the combinations are easier to remember. Its use is widespread enough that it could be used as an access point in an automated system, although the ISSN has surpassed it in universality.

The national bibliographic data base of serials is growing and its effect on serials automation is very positive. But it is hard to be patient while waiting for the retrospective compilation and verification work to be completed.

Technical improvements in computers and advances in software are lowering some costs, making networking possible and democratizing the computer revolution in libraries. But they are not, as emphasized above, lowering overall costs for the library.

The standards for library handling and describing of serials are helping. But we still need to convince publishers to follow standards in the production of their journals, proceedings, reports and other serials. We need to solve one of the weaknesses of human interaction with the computer—the identification of the serial received and the finding of the appropriate record. The ISSN and key title are helping, but a machine-readable code, such as a bar code, might be the ultimate answer. As of mid-1982, we were still waiting for the new standard on the detailed holdings statements from the Z39 Committee of the American National Standards Institute.

Great strides are being made in the control of serials. But are we prepared for the elimination of serials, as F.W. Lancaster predicts and Michael Gorman demands? We are struggling to agree on the bibliographic control of microforms. Are we ready to tackle the bibliographic control of the electronic journal?

EFFECTS OF SERIALS AUTOMATION

What is the effect of serials automation on the participants in the stream of information: the author-researcher, the editor-publisher, the librarian and the reader? Automation is helping the library control the chaos of publication, and will enable the library to give more efficient service, create better control of its collection, and fabricate better access to it. But it is not helping the library in the area of greatest need—controlling the costs of serials. Automation is improving the chance of readers to find what is wanted quickly, but it is also making them aware of more material than they can read, and there does not seem to be any solution to that problem.

The automation of serials in libraries is having little visible effect on authors and publishers. Anything that aids one part of the information nexus is good, but the short term effects looked for by authors and publishers are wanting. Automation is not releasing new money for libraries to pay for publishing activities. There is even a slight *negative* effect, for serials automation is making networking of libraries more effective and, therefore, will make further reductions in library subscriptions possible.

At least a few publishers may be very interested in the progress of library automation. These are the publishers who are considering a conversion of their paper publishing programs to electronic publication. Computer-sophisticated libraries may be potential customers for this new form of publication. Chapter 6 will deal further with the problems and prospects of electronic publishing.

FOOTNOTES

1. Dan Tonkeray, "Keynote Address" (Conference on Serials Automation, Acquisitions and Inventory Control, Milwaukee, September 4, 5, 1980; sixty-minute sound cassette from *Information Yield*).

2. Harry H. Kamens, "OCLC Serials Control Subsystem: A Case Study," *Serials Librarian* 3 (Fall 1978) :43-55.

3. Mary Matthews and Steve Sherman, "How to Computerize Your Serials and Periodicals When You Don't Know How," *Wilson Library Bulletin* 44 (April 1970) :861-64.

4. Helen H. Spalding, "A Computer-Produced Serials Book Catalog with Automatically Generated Indexes," *Library Resources and Technical Services* 24 (Fall 1980) :352-60.

5. Don Bosseau, "University of California, San Diego Serials System," Computerized Serials Systems Series, vol. 1, issue 2 (Tempe, AZ: The Larc Association, Inc., 1973) :13-25.

6. Donald P. Hammer, "Serial Publications in Large Libraries: Machine Applications," *Serial Publications in Large Libraries,* ed. Walter C. Allen, Allerton Park Institute no. 16 (Urbana: University of Illinois Graduate School of Library Science, 1970), pp. 129-131.

7. Bosseau, pp. 39-50.

8. Hammer, p. 131.

9. James Fayollat, "On-line Serials Control in a Large Biomedical Library: Part 1, Description of the System," *Journal of the American Society for Information Science* 23 (September 1972): 318-22.

10. Millard Johnson, "Subscription and Financial Functions," (Conference on Serials Automation, Acquisitions and Inventory Control, Milwaukee, September 4, 5, 1980; sixty-minute sound cassette from *Information Yield*).

11. William J. Willmering, "On-line Centralized Serials Control," *Serials Librarian* 1 (Spring 1977): 243-49.

12. "Lister Hill Integrated Library System," *Information Hotline* 13 (January 1981): 9.

13. "First Automated Library System for Under $50,000," *Information Hotline* 13 (May 1981): 11, 12.

14. Richard DeGennaro, "Libraries and Networks in Transition: Problems and Prospects for the 1980's," *Library Journal* 106 (May 15, 1981): 1048.

15. Priscilla Mayden, "The Problems of Entering a Computerized Serials Network; or The Validity of Murphy's Law," *Proceedings* of the LARC Institute on Automated Serials Systems (St. Louis: May 24-25, 1973), pp. 43-50.

16. DeGennaro, pp. 1045-49.

6

Alternative Forms of Publication

Previous chapters have examined the causes and effects of rising serials costs for both publishers and libraries. Increased publication costs have forced publishers to raise subscription rates. These, in turn, are forcing libraries to change collecting habits, cooperate with other libraries in providing materials, and seek economies through automation. Publishers are also investigating promising cost-cutting strategies.

One seemingly promising method for cutting costs of publication is to reduce printing and postage costs. This could be done in a variety of ways. One would be to send articles only to those who want to read them, not to the whole list of subscribers. Another would be to publish in a format cheaper to produce and mail than paper with ink printing. Another would be to use electronic means of storing and communicating the information. This chapter will discuss some of these alternatives.

STRENGTHS AND WEAKNESSES OF TRADITIONAL PUBLICATION

It is not easy to give up the traditional journal format. J.C.R. Licklider said, "As a medium for the display of information the printed page is superb. It affords enough resolution to meet the eye's demand. It presents enough information to occupy the reader for a convenient quantum of time. It offers great flexibility of font and format. It lets the reader control the mode and rate of inspection. It is small, light, movable, cutable, clippable, pastable, replicable, disposable, and inexpensive."[1]

Printing is well suited to mass production. Basically, the larger the number of copies printed, the cheaper each copy can be produced, since much of the cost of a print run is incurred in setting up before the first copy is printed. While labor and paper costs rose tremendously over the 500 years following Gutenberg, advances in the technology of paper making and printing helped keep costs reasonable until fairly recently. Since World War II, however, the general rise in paper and printing costs has been much greater than the general cost-of-living increases. Printing and paper costs have been a major cause of the recent precipitous increases in subscription rates.

Another advantage of printed journals was discovered by Henry Oldenburg, who created and sustained the first really successful journal, *Philosophical Transactions of the Royal Society*. Producing many copies, all duplicates of the others, saved him the labor of writing many letters to far-flung correspondents. Until recently, anyone interested in new developments in a field could keep abreast of those developments by faithful reading of the journal serving that field. But in the late 20th century, this elegant and practical solution to the problem of keeping informed is breaking down because of the overwhelming number of articles being published in a vast armada of journals. The individual, no matter how dedicated and diligent, cannot possibly read all the ones pertinent to his interests. The scholar, the teacher, the scientist and the professional are unable to keep up with their fields of interest, and libraries cannot identify, pay for or handle all the literature relevant to their users' needs.

Still another advantage of printed journals is the bibliographic control that can be given to them. Hand-copied manuscripts are unique and must be described individually. Errors are inevitable and each description will have its own, as well as perpetuating most of those of the manuscript copied. A book or journal published in hundreds of copies may also have errors, but they will be the same in each copy. Describe one copy and you describe them all. Refer to one copy and you refer to them all. Cite one copy and you cite them all. Index, abstract, quote one and you do so for all. When the reader follows up on an idea by looking up a footnoted publication, he knows he is reading the same words the author used and cited.

In the 1970s and 1980s publications may have grown beyond the capabilities of indexers and catalogers to keep up. The factor that used to be a strength of printed publications is turning into a weakness.

Publishers, authors, librarians, indexers and readers all may be reluctant to give up a medium that has worked so well, but the problems in our time are forcing them to look for alternatives.

SELECTIVE DISSEMINATION

Some libraries and commercial services have set up SDI, or selective dissemination of information, services. Such a service may photocopy tables of contents pages of selected journals and send them to individuals interested in covering those journals. Copies of the text itself may also be sent automatically.

The Institute for Scientific Information (ISI) is one of many companies that provide SDI services. A recent innovation is a service called ASCATOPICS. Designed to keep up with articles in current journals on more than 300 subjects, ASCATOPICS furnishes references only. The cost to the subscriber is $125 a year for each topic. The advantage to the reader is that the service will find articles appearing in journals not ordinarily associated with the field. Librarians, for instance, may ordinarily see the publications of the American Library Association and its divisions, but might not find articles in the scientific journals on information needs of scientists. These articles could be highly pertinent, but without ASCA-TOPICS the librarian might be very late in learning of them or never learn of them at all.

ISI also publishes many "awareness" journals—*Current Contents in Chemistry, Current Contents in Zoology* and so forth. These journals reprint tables of contents from the most important journals in their respective fields. The reader can find out about a high percentage of the most important articles in his field by subscription to a few leading journals, but would miss articles on the subject published elsewhere. The typical *Current Contents* journal covers 50 to 75 journals. The ASCATOPICS service covers 5400 journals, and gives the home address of each author to enable the reader to ask the author for a reprint directly.

Readers who want information on a particular subject within a field may ask ISI to draw up an interest profile specifically designed for their needs. This service is called Automatic Subject Citation Alert (ASCA). The cost of this service will depend on the number of citations provided.

To complete the service offered directly to readers ISI has its Original Article Tear Sheet (OATS) service, referred to in Chapter 4. Readers who learn of an article from *Current Contents, ASCA,* ASCATOPICS or other source can have their own copy sent to them for about $5. In an article published in 1974, Waldo Brooks reported on the use of the OATS service by the IBM Technical Information Retrieval Center, in Armonk, NY.[2] That center served about 3700 scientists, engineers and other IBM staff. With a projected 500 article requests per week from IBM and a 75% fulfillment rate, ISI would be sending more than 18,000 articles a year for about $95,000 at today's prices. OATS articles arrive from five to seven days following the request. For the IBM Technical Information Retrieval Center to purchase the same 5000 scientific journals covered by ISI would cost at today's prices more than $250,000.*

Selective dissemination can be a very effective and cost efficient method of putting information on the desks of readers. With little expenditure of their own time and a short elapsed time after publication date, researchers can have a high proportion of the articles relevant to their own needs. Costs are relatively low, publishers receive royalty payment from ISI for each article photocopied, and only the readers who want them receive the full texts of articles. The library is not saddled with long-term storage and maintenance expense; it can concentrate on indexing so that readers can find all they want and only what they want.

Selective dissemination of information has weaknesses, though. Publishers could not afford to print their journals solely for the income received through a service like OATS. Selective dissemination serves researchers well, but not students. Students need to read older literature, not just the current literature; moreover, they don't have filing space for reprints, money to pay for them, or the well-defined interests that can be profiled for selective dissemination. Selective dissemination works well for the identifiable key journals that publish most of the important articles, but it still cannot supply easily the articles scat-

---

*Author's calculations based on ISI price lists and Waldo E. Brooks, "How IBM's TIRC Fills Requests for Copyrighted Journal Articles," *Sci-Tech News* 28 (1974): 35-37.

tered throughout a large number of less important serial publications. The scientists who want to read the 25% of the articles that ISI cannot supply must turn to the interlibrary loan system depending on traditional libraries. Scientists whose research leads them into new subjects need to refer to older literature in those fields, which means library collections. Selective dissemination of information works for current publication, not retrospective literature. Researchers with a lifetime of SDI reports in their files will also run into the same literature problems of storage space and difficulty of indexing that libraries now have on a larger scale.

In sum, selective dissemination of information is a useful technique, especially applicable to special libraries. It supplements traditional information dissemination through journal subscriptions, but it cannot substitute for it, or cure all the problems associated with it.

ON-DEMAND PUBLICATION

Another strategy for reducing costs is to publish the availability of an article and let those who want to read it order a copy from the publisher. By various techniques the publisher can produce each copy as it is ordered.

Essentially, this method of publication differs from the selective dissemination method only slightly. In selective dissemination, the readers who are interested in an article have identified themselves before publication. They have agreed to purchase any article defined in a certain way. On-demand publication produces copies after they are ordered.

On-Demand Publication Techniques

On-demand publication depends on various simple or sophisticated technologies for economically producing one copy at a time. One method might be photocopying from a printed copy. While this is relatively inexpensive in terms of materials, its labor cost might be a deterrent. To a publisher of many articles in several journals, the filing and retrieval problems would be severe.

Microfiche or microfilm copies could be supplied more cheaply than paper copies, especially for longer articles. Microform originals can also be stored, indexed and retrieved more readily than paper. Paper copies can be made from microfilm masters on Xerox Copyflo equipment. Using this technique, University Microfilms, Inc. has produced out-of-print books on demand for years. The same system could easily be applied to journal articles, but has never caught on in the same way. (More will be said about microform as an alternative form of publication later in this chapter.)

The computer is supplying a new technique for publishing in an on-demand mode. Several devices have been made available recently that can use text in machine-readable form. At present these devices are still impractical for production of a single article, but they show potential for future small-scale application. Xerox's 9700 Electronic Printing System is the most popular of the new systems. It can be used to format and lay out a whole book, from cover to cover, integrating digitized graphics with the text. The 9700 non-impact laser printer can print at very high speeds on single 8½ x 11-inch sheets of paper.

The Imagen Company offers an on-demand printing system that uses a Canon LBP-10 tabletop laser printer. It also can take textual information from a computer system and create a variety of type fonts. Other related systems can scan graphic material and reproduce it on the Xerox 9700 printer.

A liquid crystal printing system manufactured by the Static Systems Corp. can print out in several type fonts from information typed in on the keyboard. Operators see what they have typed on a liquid crystal display. This system is available for only $6000, a price that makes on-demand printing an option that small publishers can afford.[3]

Several companies offer on-demand printing services to publishers. For example, Comvestrix and Bowne Information Service in New York, and Digital Laser Printing Services in Los Altos, CA, can take electronic text produced on word processors or computers and create printed text. Again, however, this kind of service is not yet cost effective for many publishers' needs. It is useful to the publisher who wants perhaps 50 or 100 copies of a pamphlet or book, but is still more expensive than conventional printing methods for longer runs. And it is not applicable to the journal publisher who wants to produce one or two copies of several journal articles upon request of individual readers. However, a demand cooperative publication service center for journal publishers might be cost-effective.

Economics of On-Demand Publication

If 50,000 scholarly journals stopped publication and published articles for readers on demand, how would those readers learn of the articles they wanted? One possibility would be to publish abstract journals which would describe the articles available for dissemination. These abstracting journals would be no different from *Chemical Abstracts* or *Biological Abstracts* or *Biology Digest,* or *Psychological Abstracts* or *Women's Studies Abstracts* now. Readers would be faced with the same problems they face now in sorting through all the references to find the articles valuable to them. Then they would order copies of the articles from the author, journal publisher, abstract publisher, demand publishing center or reprint supplier.

There are many questions that need to be answered about this approach. The first one relates to money. Overall costs would be reduced by publishing only copies of those articles which will be read for those who will read them, but would publishers be any better off? Would articles printed by demand produce enough revenue? The costs of printing and mailing whole journals for thousands of subscribers would be saved but still there would be many other costs. If a typical journal published 100 articles a year and the average article won 10 readers, how much would the publisher have to receive per reading to pay his editorial costs? How much would the demand printing and dissemination cost per article and how much would the reader have to pay? At what price would readers resist and do without?

Let us play a game with figures to get an idea of what we're talking about. Suppose a social science journal published quarterly has 1400 subscribers for its 450 pages of text per year. It charges $33 a year and sells 900 of its subscriptions to libraries. Its income from advertising and subscriptions is $47,500. Of that, $12,000 is spent on printing and $30,500 on other costs, including $6000 for typesetting, $7000 for professional editing, $2500 for copy editing and proofreading, $2000 for authors' honoraria, $1400 for correspondence and travel, $4000 for overhead (rent, telephone, etc.), $4000 for fulfillment (including postage) and $3600 for marketing. After costs are subtracted from revenues, the publisher realizes a profit of $5000.

By printing articles only on demand, the publisher might reduce the number of pages delivered to the typical subscriber by 75%; that is, he would supply each subscriber with 112 pages, or 11 articles, instead of 450 pages and 45 articles. He would save significant printing and fulfillment costs—about 50%, or $8000. But this represents less than 20% of his total costs. Other major costs—editorial, marketing, typesetting—would remain unaltered.

Editorial costs could be reduced by not editing articles—not an attractive solution, in many cases. Marketing costs would be lowered if the publisher could gain a higher renewal rate, thereby reducing the need to attract new subscribers. Significant savings could also be achieved by eliminating typesetting, i.e., the creation of a master for each page of the journal. This could be done by printing either from typewritten copy or author-supplied word processing discs. Assuming a cost saving of $7 per page (a cost of $6 per page, as opposed to $13 per page for typesetting), the publisher could save $3150 per year on his 450-page journal.

Thus, one way to reduce the cost of the conventional journal is to supply abstracts of 45 articles a year, eliminate typesetting and let subscribers request, on demand, 11 articles each. The saving of $11,150, deducted from total costs of $42,500, would mean that it would cost $31,350 to publish the journal and achieve the same profit of $5000. Hence, subscription cost could be lowered to ($31,350 ÷ 1400) or $22.40. Note that subscribers would be paying 66% of the previous subscription price, but receiving only 25% as many articles.

This subscription plan seems preferable to a true on-demand journal because the typical reader actually demands many fewer than 11 articles per year, out of 45 published. Let's assume that subscribers would be willing to pay $10 per year for abstracts of 45 articles, bringing an income of $14,000. The average readership of a scholarly article is said to be 10 people. If each article abstracted were subsequently purchased by 10 readers, the publisher would supply 450 articles, or 4500 pages per year. The cost would be $2250 in printing ($0.05 per page) and perhaps $1000 in fulfillment ($2.20 per article, for postage and handling). All other editorial, marketing and overhead costs will remain the same.

Thus, the publisher's printing and fulfillment costs will be $12,750 less than for the conventional journal ($3250 vs. $16,000). His total costs, after the $3150 saving on typesetting, will be $26,600 and income from the subscriptions to the abstract journal will be $14,000, leaving $12,600 to be made up from sale of articles on demand. At only 450 articles supplied, the cost for each article will have to be $28. Thus, a subscriber will pay $10 for the abstracts and $28 for one article, whereas he previously paid $33 for an entire journal! At 10 readers per article, however, the average subscriber is only ordering one third of an article per year, or one article every three years, so his average yearly bill will be $19.33 ($10 plus one third of $28). Even so, it is doubtful that many readers will choose this alternative, and the price per article it entails, over the present-day journal subscription.

To achieve a price that might be acceptable, let's say around $10 per article, the publisher will have to increase average readership significantly—perhaps five or tenfold. One hundred readers per article for an internationally distributed scholarly journal seems a modest goal, but only the most important journals achieve this readership. They are not the journals now being hurt by the cost squeeze so they are unlikely to gamble with new, hazardous publication formats.

A publisher would have incentive to include more articles in an abstract-and-demand than in the old subscription format. There would be small investment in the abstract, but each article would increase the chance of attracting paying readers. Instead of 11 articles per quarter, 50 or 100 articles could be published at an increased cost of a dollar or two per issue of the abstract journal. Ten readers per article then would come much closer to the income requirement for publishers' income.

Implications for Authors and Libraries

The mathematics might cause some of the marginal journals to try on-demand publication and if they did so, to accept many more articles for publication than they can afford to publish presently. This would help authors who cannot now find a publisher but would tend to dilute the quality of such journals and lower further the respect that articles published there would receive. The established journals, if this reasoning is correct, are less likely to change present publication practices. This would lead to a class system in publication from the author's point of view: first class is full text publication, second class is abstract-and-demand publication.

Where would libraries fit into a demand publication situation? They might be expected to subscribe to the indexes and abstracts and abstracting journals, and presumably would continue subscriptions to basic journals as long as they were published. Libraries might also purchase articles on demand for their users. If a library did that extensively and for a long time it would develop a report indexing and filing problem that would make present day cataloging backlogs seem simple. Chances are that most academic libraries would not acquire many articles in this way. In other words, the readers themselves would have to pay for almost all of the publication costs, and libraries, which provide most of the gross receipts of smaller publishers would provide very little in a demand publication situation.

MICROFORMS

The microform was a sputtering revolution that was expected to hit the library for 50 years, but it never developed. Millions of dollars have been spent on microforms in academic libraries, and they have become indispensable for many purposes in libraries. But microforms have never quite lived up to their promise.

Limited Use of Microforms

Felix Reichmann estimated in 1972 that 20% to 25% of library holdings was in microform format.[4] That is a difficult figure to verify or refute. But libraries reporting to the Association of Research Libraries tripled their microform holdings from a median 527,000 pieces in 1971-1972 to 1,354,000 pieces in 1981-1982.[5] However, microform use in most libraries is much lower than book use. This may be because of user resistance to microforms, poor cataloging, or the nature of the material libraries generally buy in microformat.

Equipment for reading film and fiche constantly improves, but is expensive. Libraries cannot afford to keep up with the newer and better models. Consequently users in most libraries are forced to use antiquated readers that hurt their eyes. They may or may not have access to a machine that will print out an image to save the user from taking lengthy notes.

Worse, libraries have accumulated microforms faster than they could be cataloged. The most valuable publications in the world won't be used if readers don't know a library has them or can't find them. Library cataloging departments nevertheless generally give microforms a lower priority than books.

It is also true that publishers have tended to use microforms most for reprinting old materials. For instance, collections of 19th century literary journals or documents about the early history of trade unions are pulled together as a package and sold to libraries. These are reprints of rare, expensive materials that few libraries could purchase in the original printed form. Libraries can purchase them at a reasonable price on microform. These materials may be important to researchers but are not likely to attract a large group of readers in most libraries no matter how good the cataloging is.

The other most common use of microforms is to publish back issues of newspapers and periodicals. This is the only feasible way for younger libraries to catch up with other institutions in holdings of back volumes of important serials. But as we are learning from library use studies, the older materials are not read as frequently as current serials. All these factors tend to make traditional library collections of 35mm microfilm, 4x6-inch microfiche, 16mm microfilm and microcards underused.

Many serials have tried publishing simultaneously in printed form and on microform. Pergamon Press offers all 350 of its journals in both paper and microfiche. Many libraries subscribe to paper and microform versions of journals. The current issues are easily browsed on paper, but instead of being bound, the paper copies are discarded, leaving the microform version as the permanent copy. While this duplicate subscription copy may be more expensive than the cost of binding, it is well worth it for many libraries that save on expensive and crowded storage space. Dual publication is not an answer to publishers' cost problems, however. Publishing in microform only would help, but there is no indication that there is any established market, libraries or individuals, that would purchase substantial numbers of subscriptions to periodicals published on microform.

New Opportunities

New technology has opened up new possibilities with microforms in the last decade, however. First came the 16mm microfilm cassette with encoded "blips" which enable automated indexing on cassette readers and reader-printers. This kind of system, developed for record management for corporations and institutions, is equally applicable for publishing. It makes the user's task much easier and tends to create a more positive feeling toward the use of microfilm.

The most interesting recent developments are the use of microforms and computers together. The older application is Computer Output Microform (COM), which films microimages of computer-produced information directly from the computer, not by filming a computer-produced printout. This technology is widely used to produce library catalogs.

Computer Assisted Retrieval (CAR) is the newer application and one which is exciting considerable interest these days. These systems marry computer and microform to provide online storage, the computer indexing and retrieving microimages from the microform "memory." An older version of this system used computer indexing to microfiles that were retrieved by the operator by hand. The new system calls for use of the encoded 16mm cartridges. Kodak, Bell and Howell, and 3M have designed readers for this new method. Micrapoint system, introduced in 1978, serves as an example of CAR. Images stored in no particular order in 16mm film cartridges are indexed by a program on floppy disks and searched through a pre-programmed "intelligent" computer. Floppy disk storage capacity is limited, and microfilm increases the storage capacity cheaply. Other similar systems use fiche, not microfilm. One study concluded that a CAR system would be less expensive as a library catalog than a computer system with total online storage would be.[6]

How could such technology be used in publishing serials? Now, while systems are being developed and there are no accepted standards, it would be very difficult for a publisher to win acceptance from subscribers for a computer-searchable microform serial publication. Once the dominant systems have won out, in a few years, it could be very advantageous for publishers to be able to send out a piece of film that would drop into a system and be instantly describable, filable and retrievable in any properly-equipped library, private home or office.

VIDEO

New developments also make the old family entertainment center into a potential document file, index, retrieval center, reader and reproduction tool.

Videotext

Of the various new technologies for providing communication, the most promising and most disappointing is videotext. Videotext can deliver information in graphic or text form from a data base to individual television sets with proper adaptors. Unlike conventional television broadcasting, the videotext information received can be selected and controlled by the viewer.

Several forms of videotext have been developed. They can be divided into two groups: 1) select-only and 2) interactive. The first allows the viewer to choose among various "pages" of information. The second allows the viewer to communicate to the computer supplying the data base and through it to other viewers or other parties. For instance, with the first system, the viewer could find out about good restaurants within 10 miles of his home. With the second, the viewer could not only read about those restaurants, but could make a reservation at one of them.

Teletext, developed by the British Broadcasting Corporation (BBC), is a one-way form of videotext. The conventional television signal is modified to make use of the "vertical blanking interval," the portion of the signal that maintains the space between the frames of the picture. Digital information is encoded into that space. In the viewer's set this information is translated into characters that can be displayed in place of the video or with it. The text is broadcast in pages, 24 lines to the page, and 40 characters to the line in the British and French versions. As long as the non-video portion of the signal is used, the signal is limited to 10,000 text characters per second. If the whole signal is devoted to text, it has the potential data rate of 5 million characters per second. The pages are cycled approximately every 15 seconds. The viewer picks out the information wanted and when that page comes through on the cycle, the set "catches" it and displays it.

The other form of videotext is called "viewdata" in the United States and Britain. Essentially, it consists of information in a computer data base, with telephone lines for transmission and television sets as display terminals. The British Post Office pioneered this system, known as Prestel in the United Kingdom. Prestel was aimed at the consumer market—that is, the information made available through Prestel was supposed to be of interest to the average household with a television set.

Videotext excites the imagination and those inclined to prophesying have been quick to pronounce it the wave of the future. So far, the uses of both teletext and viewdata in Britain have been limited, and the response of the public disappointing.

"Ceefax," the BBC teletext system, offers news headlines, summaries of late-breaking news, sports, weather, TV schedules, stock market reports and so forth. It doubles the cost of the TV monthly lease (the standard method of acquiring a television set in Britain) to the viewer. In five years, only 250,000 homes have been equipped for receiving Ceefax, a tiny fraction of the TV homes, although growth has increased in the last year. This raises questions about the information being broadcast or the information needs and habits of the public.

The Prestel service is even more of a disappointment. By the end of 1981, 14,400 sets in the United Kingdom had been registered for the system and growth was limited to about 450 sets a month.[7] Prestel was originally intended for the home user—games, quizzes and news services are most popular—but the cost made it affordable mainly to businesses. Many of them didn't need Prestel since other electronic services were already available.

From March 1981 to May 1982, the ratio of business to home users remained unchanged at 85 to 15.[8]

The French are using viewdata in several different ways. For example, some printed telephone books are being replaced by small, mass-produced terminals for a viewdata system which will provide directory assistance to customers. The Antiope videotext system developed in France is considered by some to be superior to the British system.

In the United States, several videotext experiments and projects are under way. In addition to tests conducted by various U.S. companies (e.g., CBS, AT&T, Time Inc., Knight-Ridder) Prestel service is also available. Marketing efforts are particularly strong in the U.S. since more households are equipped with telephones and televisions than in any other country in the world. But the experiment most interesting to librarians is the Channel 2000 project conducted in Columbus, OH. This may be the only viewdata experiment with a library catalog and an encyclopedia online for the home user.

Other viewdata experiments are being pursued around the world, including Canada, Germany, Japan, Denmark and the Netherlands.

Many observers remain excited about the prospects for videotext, particularly in its interactive form. Many problems remain, however, particularly with respect to cost and selection of appropriate information. Another difficulty is that videotext systems do not provide hard copy printouts, and it is uncomfortable to read more than a few pages of videotext at a time. Nevertheless, the potential exists for videotext to have a large role in the communication of information. How large that role will be, and how it will occur, will be unknown until further tests are completed.

Other Video Technologies

Other developments with television add interesting possibilities. Satellite transmission allows multivarious channels for cable TV broadcasting. Video tape cassette recorders make it possible for home viewers to save favorite programs for repeated viewing or viewing at their convenience rather than be tied to broadcast schedules. Two-way cable TV allows for viewer interaction with programmers. This creates a completely different environment for teaching and learning since the individual viewer can respond to the speaker and the speaker can respond to the individual.

Video Disc

Another new technology with dazzling possibilities is the video disc. The disc can be used to deliver feature films to the consumer at a lower price but with a better quality picture than video tape. Each disc can store 54,000 high resolution pictures on each side. Each picture could be a page of text or a graph, diagram or plate. That amounts to over a hundred 500-page volumes per side in storage and reproduction capacity. Organized another way, each side is capable of storing 20 to 30 billion bits or 2 to 3 billion characters.

Information on video discs could be indexed and manipulated further by microcomputer. Video discs can also be used to store computer memory. Information in video disc storage would be fully accessible by random access. Finally, the video disc appears to enable archival permanence superior to that of film or paper.

However, video discs, like videotext systems, have numerous problems to be resolved before they can achieve widespread use. First is the problem of incompatibility between one system and another. Second, all systems use discs that are mass produced from masters, and mastering is both costly and difficult. Third is the relatively high cost of the players, ranging from $300-$700 in spring 1982. Fourth, the home viewer cannot record programs onto a video disc, as he can with a video tape recorder. In general, it seems likely that the disc will be much more successful as an information storage medium than as a consumer product.*

COMPUTER DEVELOPMENTS

Every year the basic component of computers, the silicon microchip, becomes more sophisticated, more powerful, larger in capacity, smaller in size and energy use, and cheaper. This development has been continuing since UNIVAC with its room full of vacuum tubes was first sold in 1951. The pocket calculator is one result of this improvement in technology. Theoretically, the same components could eventually be used to produce a "book-on-a-chip," which publishers could mass produce and market for about the same price as printed books. Readers would buy them in self-contained "readers" with crystal display or could plug them in to universal readers which would be as portable as the calculator and have the same random access capability as the printed codex book. Such a product is technically possible; whether it would be useful or marketable is another—at present, unanswerable—question.

The most promising current use of computers for communications hooks them up to other computers by telecommunication. For years publishers have been abandoning hot metal typesetting and adopting computer phototypesetting machines. Vast data bases that were created in the process of indexing, typesetting or textual analysis can easily be made available for commercial use. Individuals can communicate with each other, sending messages back and forth through their computers (electronic mail). Groups of individuals at remote locations can work together to produce a document through their computers (electronic conference). Publishers can put new information in a data base and send it out through the computer network to subscribers (electronic journal). Publishers can create large data bases with indexing and text and let subscribers find the information they want, then have it printed out. This last is the computerized version of the printed loose leaf service.

Libraries have been making great use of the indexing data bases, already discussed in Chapter 4. The electronic conference, currently experimental, could become more important in the publishing process. Through this means researchers can consult with colleagues while conducting research and drafting papers. Preliminary publication, within the limited

*For a discussion of the differences between types of video discs and the prospects for their use, see Efrem Sigel, et al., *Video Discs: The Technology, The Applications and The Future* (White Plains, NY: Knowledge Industry Publications, Inc., 1980).

circle of members of the group, can be the result. Finished papers can be printed out for submission to a journal or can be sent to a publisher in machine-readable form if the publisher has the equipment to handle it that way.[9]

A more interesting possibility for the electronic conference would be its use by publishers themselves in the refereeing and editing processes. Papers could be handled more expeditiously with much better "inventory control." Editors would always know where all papers were in the process, and could easily communicate with referees and other editors, as well as production staff, no matter how remote their locations, as long as they were in the computer network. Finished papers could be set into type by the computer.

THE ELECTRONIC JOURNAL

This brings us to the journal published electronically and disseminated through telecommunication from the publisher's computer to the subscribers' computers. Once a publisher has the computer capability to edit, review, store and send messages between editors and referees and authors, why not "publish" on the computer as well?

Electronic publication would have several advantages. First, it would entail virtually no more expense to the publisher, since the subscribers would pay for transmission charges. The reports would be in the computer already. No other expensive step need be taken to print or microfilm or reproduce from the publisher's master. Second, it could allow the publisher to accept many reports now rejected only because of lack of space. With the ever-increasing computer memories at decreasing prices, publishers could generously accept all worthy articles submitted without increasing costs of publication. Third, the data base could be made available to secondary publishers for indexing and abstracting more rapidly and could then incorporate the indexers' terms. Fourth, the readers' comments after reading could be recorded. In a short time, certain articles would cumulate many reactions that would identify their importance for later readers. Since these would be dated, it would also show declining use of older materials or even the later appreciation for "rediscoveries." Fifth, the electronic publication of journals would make possible the recording of citations by later authors. Readers would be led through the literature from author to author by these connections.

One problem with this plan is that most potential subscribers lack the computer to receive, file and manipulate an electronic journal. In certain subject fields, however, almost every "subscriber" should have access to computers. Computer science is an obvious example. A very high percentage of potential subscribers in most of the hard sciences and in engineering disciplines would also have computer access and would constitute adequate audiences for several journals in those fields. Another hurdle preventing easy adoption of electronic publication is the problem of incompatibility of computers, but this problem is yielding to the rapid development in computer sophistication and the software packages that translate between systems. The library may have a role to play here, supplying a central "receiving station" and storage for electronic journals for local users, much like the role libraries play with printed journals. The cost of high-speed communication, not the computer hook up itself, may be the crucial problem for the ordinary user—which creates the need for the library.[10]

Several electronic serials publications now exist. One example is the research journals of the American Chemical Society, which are now available online through the Bibliographic Retrieval Services. BRS has developed new searching software that allows users to search the text itself, not just the article titles or abstracts.[11]

Pergamon Press took over ownership of the British computer-based retrieval service InfoLine Limited and is developing online information services. That could lead to many more electronic journals.[12] Through InfoLine, Pergamon offers VIDEO PATSEARCH, an online system for retrieval of information on patents. The pictures or drawings contained in the patents are stored on video discs and are accessible through a microcomputer-controlled video disc player.

Several computer-assisted legal research systems are available to help judges, lawyers and law students do legal research. LEXIS was developed by Mead Data Central under a contract with the Ohio Bar Association. In 1973 Mead began marketing LEXIS nationwide. West Publishing Co. developed WESTLAW as a roughly equivalent service. Both provide state appellate opinions, federal court opinions, U.S. Supreme Court opinions, the *U.S. Code* and other materials. JURIS, FLITE and AUTO-CITE are other more limited systems. All allow the user to find relevant citations and the full text of those citations. Although very expensive, the quality of the results appears to be winning new converts to the systems.[13] In 1979 it was estimated that 600 subscribers used LEXIS and about 100 used WESTLAW. Increased use of the computer-assisted legal research systems appears inevitable. It may be necessary to create new methods of paying for the service. Cooperative sharing of terminals between smaller firms appears promising, especially if a research specialist is available to conduct or aid in the search.

Another full-text transmission system was tested and proved technically feasible in an experiment in 1978 and 1979. The American Institute of Physics (AIP) and Applied Communication Research, Inc. conducted the project on a National Science Foundation grant. The aim was to "test the technical feasibility of an analog-based electronic journal system that combined online identification of relevant documents with facsimile transmission of those documents on request."[14] The experiment also tested the utility of transmission of data with a communication satellite. Despite some technical problems, the system worked perfectly.

Surprisingly, in three of the four libraries participating in the test, very few patrons used the system or even seemed to be aware of it. In other words, the system worked, but it failed in that people who had free access to it did not use it. In large part, this was because the libraries already subscribed to the journals most of the patrons needed, and there was no need for them to ask for a sophisticated satellite-transmitted facsimile of the article they could simply find on the shelf. The results are disappointing, but instructive. The electronic journal is feasible technically, but has not yet proved that it can replace the printed journal. If it was not accepted by those who had the service free, how will people who pay connect-time, data base charges and text printout page charges accept it? Is the electronic journal economically feasible?

WILL THE ELECTRONIC JOURNAL PAY FOR ITSELF?

We end where we started. How can we transmit information in such a way that the producers receive a fair return and the consumers of information are willing to pay for what they receive?

We can divide information into four rough categories: entertainment, news and comment, scholarly and creative expression. If the population of the United States is about 220 million people, the market for entertainment corresponds roughly to the total population minus infants (and those "cranks" who refuse to have a television set in the house)—let's say about 200 million people. (The average Sunday night television audience is 100 million.) With that kind of mass audience, producers can spend millions of dollars on one show and have an excellent chance of recouping their investment. With that kind of audience, it is possible to experiment with new means of delivery and packaging of information. The millions of dollars spent developing video disc technology is speculative but may pay off handsomely (although current sales are disappointing). The investments in cable TV and satellite transmission to cable systems have already made many millionaires.

The second category of information, news and comment, has nearly as large an audience. Let us arbitrarily assume that the population with a high school education is roughly equivalent to the potential consumer population for news. That would total about 150 million people. In 1975, it is estimated that 61,222,000 copies of daily newspapers were circulated. The average household is 2.9 persons, so those 61 million newspapers would be reaching more than 175 million people. With an audience that large, the enormously expensive job of seeking out, writing, printing and distributing millions of words of text can be accomplished while each consumer of the newspaper pays a very small amount.

There are many sub-categories of the news and comment category. Each of the professions and hobby and consumer interest groups has an interest in specialized news. These are the groups served by newsletters and the growing trade and consumer magazines. The size of these separate markets fluctuates greatly, depending on the size of the group, the relative dedication to the subject and the amount of discretionary income available to them. For instance, there are probably as many cameras in the United States as there are households, but only a few million have fine cameras capable of taking quality pictures. Those two or three million will support several photography magazines. More households are on welfare than have 35 mm cameras, but because of the difference in discretionary income, the market for consumer magazines aimed at mothers receiving aid to dependent children is not promising.

The most affluent of the specialized populations interested in news are the very small groups of people in business. To these groups, information is an investment with a direct return, sometimes received immediately (stock market predictions), sometimes with long-term payoff (product research and development). The very high priced newsletters find their select readers from among these people.

The third kind of information, scholarly studies, has an audience more or less the size of the faculty of institutions of higher learning in the U.S.: 851,000 individuals in 1982. We may admit that some active scholars are not employed by universities, and that graduate students also constitute, however reluctantly, part of the audience for scholarly publications. The skeptic may reply that many faculty members and perhaps more graduate students do not read scholarly literature, but repeat what they learned years ago and satisfy course requirements for a degree, respectively. Nevertheless, we might add to the 851,000 figure the number of graduate students enrolled in American universities: 1,525,000. The total audience then reaches 2,376,000 or 1% of the population of the United States.

According to Derek De Solla Price, knowledge is organized into about 3000 subspecialties, with about 300 active reader-authors working in each. Worldwide, he projects about 1 million authors of scholarly papers.[15] The economic prospect of creating 3000 separate "journals" or information circuits nourishing 300 readers each is not good. Even if we admit that for every author of scholarly literature, there are ten readers who would like to write but never will, we still have only 3000 readers per subspecialty in the United States. Whether we use Price's figures, or our own, the size of the audience for scholarly information is quite small in comparison to the audience for entertainment. Therefore, we must be most careful in projecting the revolutionary use of expensive new technologies that show brilliant potential for entertainment for the transmission of scholarly information.

The audience for creative expression, such as novels, short stories, poetry and plays, is likewise limited. It goes without saying that this audience will not support electronic alternatives to print, unless they are audiovisal—e.g., movies, television, video cassettes.

The increase in print costs is remorseless. Sooner or later, many or most of the scholarly journals will have to find some suitable alternative to the present system. It seems likely that for some years there will be a mix of printed journals and electronic journals. As Donald King points out, the larger publishers tend to be successful with the present system and have little incentive to adopt electronic publishing. For one thing, payment for use of electronic information comes as a royalty, after the investment by the publisher has been made. Payment for printed journals comes in before the investment, reducing the capitalization costs and the risk.[16] That the smaller journal publishers will have the most incentive to change is a deterrent to speedy change. Change takes money, and the smaller publishers are most likely to be undercapitalized.

Because of these factors, we can expect many journals to go under before smooth progression from print to electronic publication is accomplished. Because of these factors, we can expect many difficulties with new electronic journals because shoestring operations are more likely to have problems of consistency. They are less likely to be able to afford standardization or to be able to respond to the needs of libraries and the secondary publications that create bibliographic control. We shall pursue these effects and project some trends for the next few years in scholarly communication in the next chapter.

FOOTNOTES

1. J.C.R. Licklider, *Libraries of the Future* (Cambridge: M.I.T. Press, 1965), p. 4.

2. Waldo E. Brooks, "How IBM's TIRC Fills Requests for Copyrighted Journal Articles," *Sci-Tech News* 28 (1974): 35-37.

3. Roloyn Shotwell, "Books on Demand—2: What's Happening Now," *Publishers Weekly* 219 (June 5, 1981): 50-52.

4. Felix Reichmann, "Bibliographic Control of Microforms," *Microform Review* 1 (October 1972): 279.

5. *Academic Library Statistics 1970-71* (Washington, DC: Association of Research Libraries, 1972), p. [6] and *ARL Statistics 1980/81* (Washington, DC: Association of Research Libraries, 1982): p. 18.

6. Robert M. Hayes, "On-Line Microfiche Catalogs," *Journal of Micrographics* 13 (March-April 1980): 15-33, 58-63.

7. *Videotex—Key to the Information Revolution* (Middlesex, UK: Online Publications Ltd., 1982), p. 530.

8. Ibid.

9. Tom R. Featheringham, "Computerized Conferencing and Human Communication," *IEEE Transactions on Professional Communication,* vol. PC-20, no. 4 (December 1977): 207-213.

10. Richard C. Roistacher, "The Virtual Journal: Reaching the Reader," in Clinic on Library Applications of Data Processing (proceedings 1980), *The Role of the Library in an Electronic Society* (Urbana: University of Illinois Graduate School of Library Science, 1980), p. 19.

11. *Advanced Technology/Libraries* 10 (April 1981): 8.

12. *Information Retrieval and Library Automation* 16 (July 1980): 1.

13. For a summary of the history and current state of the art of computer-assisted legal research, see Signe E. Larson and Martha E. Williams, "Computer Assisted Research," in *Annual Review of Information Science and Technology* (White Plains, NY: Knowledge Industry Publications, Inc., 1980), pp. 251-286; and Fred M. Greguras, "Legal Research," in *Online Search Strategies,* Ryan E. Hoover, ed. (White Plains, NY: Knowledge Industry Publications, Inc., forthcoming).

14. Rita G. Lerner, Colin K. Mick and Daniel Callahan, *Database Searching and Document Delivery Via Communications Satellite, Final Report to the National Science Foundation* (New York: American Institute of Physics, 1980), p. 12.

15. Derek De Solla Price, "Happiness is a Warm Librarian," in Clinic of Library Applications of Data Processing (proceedings 1980), *The Role of the Library in an Electronic Society* (Urbana: University of Illinois Graduate School of Library Science, 1980), p. 13.

16. Donald W. King, "Roadblocks to Future Ideal Information Transfer Systems," in *Telecommunications and Libraries, a Primer for Librarians and Information Managers* (White Plains, NY: Knowledge Industry Publications, Inc., 1981), p. 161.

7

Issues and Recommendations

The serials explosion has given rise to a number of issues, some philosophical, others practical, which publishers and libraries must resolve. This chapter will discuss the major issues and offer some recommendations that might lead to an improvement in the current system. Such improvement is vital, because the system in operation today is failing readers, authors, editors, publishers and libraries.

As we have discussed, the serial differs from the book by creating a definable community which receives and reads and to some extent writes for it. One or two issues create the expectation for a third and a fourth. Because of that community, authors have a ready-made audience for their writings. But the proliferation of knowledge and of scholarly writing has apparently reached the point of information overload. Readers can't keep up with all the articles written on subjects of interest to them. These articles are scattered throughout hundreds of journals. The reader can't find out about them or retrieve copies of them, let alone read and digest them. Meanwhile the journals that are most central to the research interests of the individual scholar only publish a small number of articles per year of great interest to him. The rest of the articles may be scanned quickly or ignored. The journal system is failing readers.

Since readers are not able to find all the relevant articles, those articles are not being read by the audience that could use them. This means that the people whom the author is writing for are not receiving the message. The journal system is failing authors.

The literature is so scattered that editors cannot possibly keep up with all of it either. How then can they know whether an article being considered has been published already in another form by another journal, either by the same or another author? Without effective control of the quality of the scholarly writing being published, the value of scholarly publications is reduced. More citations need to be checked by readers but fewer original papers of value are discovered. The journal system is failing editors.

Costs of publications are rising at a faster rate than most publishers can absorb or recover them. Many honest, important journals of consequence with smallish subscription lists are faced with debt or bankruptcy. Other publishers succeed because they give up scholarship in favor of more saleable content. At the same time, all publishers are losing control of what they have published because photocopiers are cheap and ubiquitous. The journal system is failing publishers.

The publishers who are successfully riding out the storm of inflation rely heavily on high institutional subscription rates charged to libraries. Libraries are being squeezed at a time when budgets have lost elasticity. Private colleges are hurt by the lowered ability of benefactors to give them funds. Public colleges are hurt by taxpayer revolts and lowered revenues in economically troubled times. Libraries are forced to cut subscriptions, stop purchasing books or both. At the same time libraries have difficulty serving readers who need a wider and wider range of journals. They are more dependent on interlibrary loans, but the administrative burden of interlibrary loans is itself becoming intolerable. The journal system is failing libraries.

Indexers, too, have difficulties with the wide scattering of publication, but proliferation and scattering make indexes indispensable to the scholarly community. Indexers and publishers of secondary publications have solved many of their problems with the computer. First used to drive a typesetting photocompositor by an indexer (*Index Medicus*), the computer has almost completely taken over book and journal typesetting. The information produced for print was simultaneously put in machine-readable form and in this form was easily used by indexers to make cumulations and create different points of access to the file of information. The computer typesetter led to the computerized information data base as primary and secondary publishers found new ways to market the machine-readable information they created. The journal system has served indexers very well, and indexers are serving the journal system well through the use of the computer.

This is now our situation: a system in disarray but with a new technology promising miraculous solutions in the near future. However, this marvelous technology will not solve every problem instantly. Let us consider some of the issues raised in the first six chapters, and suggest a few solutions.

THE KNOWLEDGE EXPLOSION

Is knowledge really expanding or is the explosion of publication merely the result of self-serving careerism of university faculty? From the historical perspective the growth of knowledge has been steady, and what we are experiencing is consistent with the number of scholars and scientists who are engaged in research. Some writing is derivative and weak; some writing is fraudulent or plagiarized; and some is creative and descriptive about subjects so specialized that no one else in the world is interested. However, there is no reason to believe it has ever been different. Poor writing and research proliferate, but they do not impede the progress of knowledge.

Nearly every scholarly study proposes subjects for further study. Each advance uncovers several areas that we don't know enough about. What we learn is like a sphere. As it expands, the surface worked by scholars grows. Think of it as a mine. The face of the exposed bedrock of the unknown grows as we mine it. Some surfaces are more resistant than others. Some brilliant researchers work far ahead of others creating new branches into the unknown, while some more plodding, more ordinary workers clean up the less interesting problems left behind.

If the expansion of knowledge is real, is it responsible for us to make it more difficult to publish? Should we allow the less viable journals to die as DeGennaro proposes? Yes, the free marketplace for publication places some check on the proliferation of undeserving or second-rate research. If any research could be published freely, we would have a more difficult time yet in culling the good from the bad.

The computer, the microform, the abstract journal and perhaps other alternative forms of publication are likely to create a solution of sorts for us. In the foreseeable future we are likely to have a mix of publications, much as we have now. Fewer journals will survive in paper, but the strongest will. Those which can attract the income to pay for print will continue to publish that way because of the subscription advantages to publishers and because of reader preference for paper. Those journals with large numbers of personal subscribers will continue to sell to libraries; those with sales to libraries only will not find enough income to continue. Various forms of publication, such as abstract journals with on-demand publication support, microform journals, video disc journals and electronic journals will emerge. Some will be refereed and will have large and small audiences with personal and institutional subscriptions. Some will be collections of reports, speeches and studies, like the ERIC reports and NTIS.

Authors will be presented with a three-tiered system of publication in such a system. The greatest prestige will come from publication in the printed journals. Next best will be the refereed publications with less expensive publication mode and smaller readership. Least prestigious, but still better than not publishing, will be the catch-all collections. Some gems will be found in these, but much will have little interest to any but the most thorough of future researchers. Fortunately, the capacity of the computer to index all this material will mean none of it will be lost to future readers.

COSTS

The second major issue is the cost of serials. We know that publishers' costs are rising. But is it legitimate for publishers to charge libraries two, five or ten times as much as individual subscribers are charged? Could a publisher justify 20, 50 or 100 times the individual rate for a subscription to a consortium? Should librarians acquiesce in this money-making strategy from any publisher or should distinctions be made between profit and not-for-profit publishers?

A publisher's attitude toward libraries probably depends upon the size of the publisher's subscription list and his perception of the future potential of his list. The publisher with millions of subscribers is indifferent to libraries, treating them like any other subscribers and charging them no more for their subscriptions, even though 75% of the fulfillment problems come from libraries.

The publisher of a fairly new periodical with a growing list of thousands of subscribers is likely to court the business of libraries. A library subscriber is a recommendation—like a positive review. Library readers will discover the magazine and many of them will want their own copies. These publishers will also be inclined to charge libraries no more than individual subscribers and are more likely to offer good discounts (20%) to subscription agents.

A publisher of a scholarly journal who is dependent on libraries for a substantial portion of his income will tend to charge much more for institutional than for individual subscriptions.

Serials librarians may be bewildered by these variations. Librarians may as well adjust to higher subscription prices and to the institutional rate. There appears to be no legal limit to the price a publisher can charge libraries, and perhaps none should be sought. The marketplace is probably the best regulator.

One proposal raised by publishers is to levy "usage charges" on libraries. Every time a reader checked out a book or asked for a periodical, the library would be bound to pay a reading fee to the publisher. Such a scheme would be likely to help a few publishers of the most popular materials at the expense of the rest. The libraries would spend much more on record keeping and would be less able to purchase books and serials.

Any scheme to increase publishers' income from libraries is bound to fail, say most librarians, because libraries have only a limited amount of money available to spend. The more costs of publications rise the fewer of them libraries will be able to buy. This brings on the familiar tailspin effect of fewer subscriptions, higher prices, fewer subscriptions, etc.

Some individual publishers may do well in this situation. But it is clear that publishers as a whole must cut costs, find new sources of income, or go out of business. New sources of income seem unlikely now. Many serial publishers, it seems, must cease publication in the next decade, reversing a trend that has been continuing since 1655. More and more of those who survive will do so because they are able to utilize the new electronic technology to save costs.

PHOTOCOPYING AND COPYRIGHT

The copyright law of 1976 has been a disappointment to publishers. It seems likely that any revisions to it will be minor ones, however. For instance, libraries may be given more detailed guidance on their obligations under the copyright law for putting copied materials on reserve for assigned reading. Even without further legislation, it appears likely that any viable national library consortium will negotiate with publishers a fee payment for photocopies or uses. Whatever changes are made will probably not significantly increase publishers' income. That source of income that seemed so promising to publishers four years ago now must be written off.

One surprising development with the copyright law was the ruling by the three-judge panel of the United States Court of Appeals for the Ninth Circuit in San Francisco on

October 19, 1981. It ruled that the use of video tape recorders violated the copyright law because owners of recorders are gaining "economic control" over the copyrighted works that were broadcast. The suit was brought by two Hollywood movie studios, Walt Disney Productions and Universal City Studios. In 1979 Federal Judge Warren J. Ferguson ruled against the plaintiffs, but the Court of Appeals ruling sent the case back to him and ordered him to fashion some kind of relief for the damage done to the plaintiffs by video recorders. The Sony Corporation, manufacturer of the Betamax, will probably appeal to the Supreme Court.[1]

If this decision is not reversed, it will certainly hurt the sale of video recorders for the home market. Some kind of royalty charge could be included in the purchase price of recorders which would be paid to producers of broadcast shows, although it is hard to imagine how the royalties would be divided among all eligible producers and produce any income at all. The total pool would be required just to administer the program—a situation closely parallel to that of the Copyright Clearance Center. The producers are trying to maintain the market for video cassettes for themselves, and don't expect to receive income from the sale of video recorders. They would prefer that no home video recorders exist. On the other hand, they would like to see millions of video players in homes as a market for their cassettes.

It is chancy to predict the possible effects of this development on serials, but they could be far-ranging. For instance, if the court decision prevails, it could give video disc players a boost, since the major advantage of the tape recorder is that broadcast material can be recorded, while video disc players cannot record. If the courts prohibit free videotaping, the cheaper price and better quality of video discs may give them the advantage. A better market for video discs could make them a better future medium for serial-type publications. On the other hand, if the Appeals Court decision stands, it may take away some of the possible configurations for transmitting and using entertainment in the future, and with it could be swept away the means for publishing scholarly information in some electronic formats.

ACCESS TO INFORMATION

The computer is creating an access problem for librarians as it creates new and better access to published literature. As its role enlarges, those seeking information become more dependent on the computer to provide it. Since the computer makes the user totally dependent on technology, it creates a means of controlling who has access to the information. The computer has also introduced a new fee-for-service precedent into American libraries that not only limits free access for some specialized services, but could spill over to become the standard relationship between library and user. To some people this is one of the most disturbing of recent developments. Others urge that it is merely a necessary adaptation of the old tax-based library book service to the needs of a modern information-based society.

Libraries have purchased millions of copies of books and serials and made them available to the citizens and guests of America. Each book and serial is a capital investment already paid for by the library for which no reimbursement is necessary. Each book has relatively low value as a physical object and can be turned over to the complete control of the user with relatively limited safeguards. Anyone with the ability to read can make full use of these printed materials with limited library staff mediation. Because many different readers need many different books, and the flow of materials from user to library to user is promoted by loan periods, libraries are able to serve thousands of readers at the same time.

Computers change all that. If the same information is in a computer instead of in printed books and serials, the library must buy equipment to make that information available. This equipment must be protected from misuse. The use of the computer equipment requires staff assistance (ironically, using the computer in public service in the library is much more labor intensive than the book). The library can help only those people who have a computer to use, and the institution may not be able to afford enough to avoid queues and waiting lists. Users will have to learn the skill of manipulating a computer or depend on an expert to do it for them. The computer will create a new form of illiteracy and dependency. The computer could also be used to invade privacy or to control information available to certain users. This misuse of the computer would be particularly sinister because it could be done from remote locations and without the knowledge of its victims.

If that sounds alarmist and fantastic, another mechanism introduced by computers is all too real. Computer searches of online data bases cost money. In most libraries, all or part of the fee charged by the bibliographic search service is passed on to the user. This is no procedural aberration or temporary policy, and it threatens to change radically the nature of library service.

The publisher of printed serials is paid largely in advance by subscription. The book publisher is paid as stocks of the book sell—whether anyone reads the book or not. The book and serial publishers are paid when someone acquires the paper copy, not when someone uses it.

The computer works naturally on a different basis. The information in the memory of the computer is not usable until retrieved. The companies controlling the computer information bank receive their money when someone interacts with the computer and retrieves some of the information. With the computer as medium, publishers will expect to be paid for each *reading* of their copyrighted material, not for original purchase. When libraries make information from computer data banks available to readers, publishers think of libraries as retailers of the information and expect payment.

This has become, in the past few years, the cause of considerable controversy among librarians. Many, if not most, libraries do pass on the hookup and printout charges for online computer searches, but not staff time. (Most libraries also pass on interlibrary loan charges initiated by lending libraries.) A vociferous group of librarians has discovered that the fees collected by libraries, no matter how reasonable, or by whom originated, create a new class system of information users and change entirely the relationship of library to user.

Classes of Information Users

Already one can say that three "classes" of information users exist. The "upper" class are those fortunates whose employers provide nearly unlimited access to information through expensive, elaborate, up-to-date computers, word processors and telecommunications. Those people without such an employer but who can themselves afford to pay for home computers and entertainment centers constitute a "lower upper" class. They can or soon will be able to obtain online services and packages. They can buy video tapes, video discs and perhaps even satellite receiving antennas. These are the equivalent of the "idle rich." While they can afford expensive information, they may spend their money on expensive equipment in order to play computer games, or be surfeited with more broadcast options than their friends. The "upper upper" class uses information for its cash value. Such people use the services of professional programmers and computer operators, as well as the latest, most powerful equipment.

At the other end of the scale in our information-rich society is the "lower" class, defined not by automobile, or clothing or access to a bathtub, but by inability to afford an information center. Prognosticators say that in 10 years every home will have its own home computer, just as "nearly everyone" now owns a pocket electronic calculator. But surely some in our society will buy food rather than a computer if they cannot afford both. Some will decline to purchase a computer unless it comes free with a TV set. In one view, these lower class untouchables could also be defined by their use of information. As long as they have use only for entertainment, they will remain lower class.

The middle class, to complete the simile, is the herd of people in between: they want information, but can afford only a limited information center at home. Perhaps they will play recordings on cassette or video disc, but they cannot afford online remote hookups. These are the people who will turn to the library to provide information. They will be able to pay for library services.

The lower class will be shut out by their inability to pay. They are not so destitute now, when much of the information they need is available in the library in printed form at no cost. As printed publications die out and are replaced by electronic ones, the lower class will be impoverished to a greater extent.

This description of social classes defined by their access to electronic information appears to be farfetched. But isn't the library now making a distinction between persons based on their ability to pay? Don't those who cannot pay the fee constitute a "lower" class without the access to information that their "betters" can enjoy?

In the university we already have the class system. Most faculty in the sciences are now upper class, and others are middle class. Students tend to be middle or lower class. If the pay-for-use configuration becomes the rule, colleges and universities might be judged by the percentage of faculty and students who are upper versus middle class information users. (It would, of course, be scandalous to have any lower class users.)

Libraries as Fee Collectors

Libraries may be asked to expand their role as fee collectors. William Koch of the American Institute of Physics wants libraries to be partners in publishing.[2] "Republishers," he calls them. He reviews the tension that exists now between publisher and librarian and locates the problem. It is the librarians' insistence on interpreting the "fair-use" language in the 1976 copyright law as a general principle, not as a rare exception. The solution he finds is for publishers to stop being suspicious and to accept librarians as the necessary distributors of their publications, who broaden their readership and have closer relationships with the readers than the publishers do. The publishers should accept libraries as "republishers" who will furnish readers with copies of their journals for a price and who will turn back a portion of the fee to the copyright owners.

Librarians will see no reason to change their policies toward photocopying printed journals on the basis of Koch's article. Read it again in the light of the electronic journal, and it begins to make a different kind of sense. Libraries collect fees and pay computer data base owners now, don't they? If they arranged for document retrieval, either for a photocopy via interlibrary loan or a facsimile reprint via satellite, they would collect a fee, wouldn't they?

In the latter part of the 20th century, information is increasingly becoming a commodity to be developed, controlled, protected, bought and sold, like wheat, tin and bauxite. The scholarly attitude toward information is that it is beneficial to all mankind and should be freely accessible to all. The new value system, some say, reflects the values of corporations —and in our time more corporations are producing information, not manufactured goods, and use Ph.D.s, not hard hats, as a labor force.

On the other hand, it is precisely *because* information is increasingly important in our society that the fundamental idea of information as property is beneficial to authors and researchers. Their interests are protected, not denied, by the operations of the marketplace. The corporations that employ researchers, and the data bank producers and publishers who disseminate their work, are making money as a result—but how else would the author/scholar be recompensed for his labors? Would we prefer to see a "super foundation," perhaps government-sponsored, supporting our authors and scholars? Would this contribute to freedom of information generation and access? Or would it give rise to the greater threat of information censorship and control?

Some librarians believe that publishers of scholarly journals should think like scholars, not businessmen. But publishers *are* businessmen—and, as we have seen, must be in order to survive.

This realization, however, does not make the library's fee-versus-free services problem any easier to solve. Librarians may believe in free access to printed information, but there is no easy way to avoid fees for computer searches. Suppose that a university analyzes the use of a bibliographic search service and the growth of that service in its library. Let us say that more than 1300 searches were performed in 1980 at an average cost of $10, while 1000 searches were performed in 1979. Let's suppose the library administration decides to put $17,000 in the budget to fund searches without charge to users. The $17,000 allows for growth of the service, inflation and a little over for the unexpected. We can guess that the funds would be expended before midyear. Without the fees to create restraint, users would conduct more and longer searches. It would be like furnishing free Xerox copies. No amount of machines would prove adequate to supply the demand.

The library could adopt rules about the number of searches any user could request per year or the maximum length of printouts, or could pay for the first $10 per search but collect any charges incurred over that. All these rules would help spread the money, but all would impose record-keeping problems and a bureaucratic atmosphere. Some students would contrive to get around the rules. We might also suppose that in 1982, 2000 freshmen would turn up requesting searches after they heard about the service. Would the library have to adopt rules defining what class of student is eligible for the free computer searches? The library could easily find itself in an administrative morass in its attempt to maintain the democratic ideal of free access to all.

Vendors of information have a virtual monopoly, since almost all of it is unique, or at least packaged uniquely. Whereas one entertainment can replace another with little difficulty (does anyone care that "Count Your Dollars" is cancelled and replaced by "Name That Price"?), reports of scholarly research are or should be all unique, if not invaluable. Payment for access is inherently distasteful if some students or scholars are thereby denied access to relevant information, but is there any other way to set up a computer-based information service?

An Electronic Journal by Subscription?

I propose that libraries and publishers should examine this problem and work toward an acceptable alternative to pay-for-each-access. For instance, the publisher could establish an annual fee for an electronic journal. This fee would give unlimited access (including reproduction rights) to the library and its patrons for a year and would be paid in advance. The library could easily cancel at the end of the year and the publisher could set whatever price seemed reasonable for the following year. During a subscription year the library would have access to the current year only, or for a higher fee, could have access to past years as well. If a library cancelled its subscription, it would lose access to the years it had already subscribed to. (Alternatively, the library could purchase permanent access to volumes and still have that access after cancelling its current subscription. It could pull the "volumes" purchased from the publisher's data base and enter it into the library's local online system.)

If the subscription price could be agreed on, this arrangement would have advantages for both. Publishers would have the old advantage of publishing serials—money in advance. They would also have some guarantee that the product would bring in a certain income, rather than worrying about the saleability of each article. Libraries would have the benefit of being able to offer access to anyone and would be in the position of encouraging use rather than discouraging it. Each use would make the subscription a better bargain for the library.

This arrangement would work to the advantage of readers, also, since no artificial barriers would be raised between them and the information they need. Since it would tend to promote a wider audience, authors would benefit also. This arrangement would also work for authors by giving publishers no incentive to seek only popular or "best selling" articles as the other system would tend to do.

STANDARDIZATION

One of the most exasperating problems for librarians is the needless extra work caused by serials with unusual numbering systems, hidden bibliographic information, unannounced title changes, and other vagaries. What may seem a creative solution to a publisher is a headache to librarians and indexers who must deal with thousands of publications and create bibliographic control for them, as we discussed in Chapter 3. As long as the serial is viewed by its publisher as a private commodity for sale to the public, the problems librarians have with it are irrelevant. But when the journal is a unit in a national and international system of information exchange, the situation changes. The publisher has an obligation to produce the journal in a format that fits smoothly into that system.

The International Serials Data System has been an encouraging success. International Standard Serial Numbers (ISSN) have been assigned to thousands of serials all over the world, with a high percentage of publishers in England, Scandinavia, other European countries, Canada and the United States participating. The U.S. Postal Service requires that periodicals follow certain rules in order to qualify for second class mailing privileges. These rules have been very helpful to librarians. Because of them we know approximately on what page the bibliographic data will appear. Thus, a well-trained clerk who finds no volume and issue numbers on the cover can usually find them on page 3, 4 or 5 (or 6, 7 or 8) along with the publisher's address, the frequency of publication and the subscription rate.

It would come as a surprise to many publishers (and librarians) that sets of standards exist governing the publication of periodicals. Among existing standards are the "International Standard Recommendation for the Layout of Periodicals," ISO/R8-1954, the "British Standard Specification for the Presentation of Serial Publications, including Periodicals," BS 2509-1970, and the "American National Standard for Periodicals: Format and Arrangement," ANS1 Z39.1-1977.

The last publication is a standard that was first written in 1939 and has been revised several times since then, most recently in 1977. It says about itself: "An American National Standard implies a consensus of those substantially concerned with its scope and provisions. An American National Standard is intended as a guide to aid the manufacturer, the consumer, and the general public."[3]

The recommendations of the standard cover a surprising number of items and possibilities. They can be listed in the following areas:

1. *Title.* Five recommendations (keep it short, unique, "define as precisely as possible the special field of knowledge dealt with," etc.)

2. *Cover and spine.* 12 recommendations ("front cover . . . should contain . . . title, . . . subtitle, if any, . . . number of the volume and number of the issue . . . date of the issue . . . International Standard Serial Number . . . location of the table of contents," etc.)

3. *Table of Contents.* 12 recommendations ("Each issue should contain a table of

contents with . . . bibliographic information . . . information on individual articles," etc.)

4. *Masthead.* 11 recommendations ("Containing . . . title and subtitle, with ISSN . . . publisher with full address . . . editor or editorial staff," etc.)

5. *Pages.* 11 recommendations ("Each double-page spread . . . should carry the bibliographic data necessary for the rapid identification of the periodical issue, . . . including title . . . volume and issue numbers . . . page number," etc.)

6. *Articles appearing in installments.* Seven recommendations (For instance, "all installments of an article should be within a single volume, preferably in consecutive issues.")

7. *Instructions to authors.* Two recommendations ("The location of instructions to authors should be the same from issue to issue," etc.)

8. *Supplements.* Four recommendations ("A supplement should conform in trim size and page characteristics to the parent periodical," etc.)

9. *Volumes.* Eight recommendations ("A volume when completed should include: . . . a title page . . . tables of contents . . . text . . . a volume index," etc.)

10. *Changes or irregularities.* 10 recommendations ("If the size of a periodical must be altered. . . . If the title of a periodical must be changed. . . . If two or more periodicals are amalgamated . . .," etc.)

11. *Translation Periodicals.* One recommendation ("should carry, in addition to the translation title, the title in the original language . . .")[4]

The casual observer is surprised by the variations and possibilities covered. Even the experienced serials librarian is hard put to find problems not covered by the standard. All the problems librarians experience, or almost all of them, seem to be covered.

The ANSI standard on periodicals is gratifying but also frustrating to librarians. The problems would disappear if publishers would only follow the standard—but they don't. The noncompliance of publishers appears to be the standard's greatest weakness. What good does it do if the standard is improved every five years or so but publishers either don't know about it or ignore it?

As a matter of fact, the standard is written with the knowledge that it may not be followed in detail by most publishers. "The existence of an American National Standard does not in any respect preclude anyone, whether he has approved the standard or not, from manufacturing, marketing, purchasing, or using products, processes, or procedures not conforming to the standard."[5] The committee realized in writing the standard that different publishers have quite different needs. ". . . the problems of consumer and trade publications often differ considerably from those of scholarly publications. Rather than present two separate standards, however, the subcommittee agreed that a single document giving detailed and in some cases seemingly repetitive statements would be most useful.''

I have never seen a periodical that adhered to the standard in every particular. Most scholarly journals follow almost every recommendation, but will reject (or neglect) one. Few list the page of the table of contents on the front cover. Those that do will leave the ISSN number off of the table of contents page or the masthead or will leave out some bibliographic detail from the running title. None of these cause serious problems to the librarian, the indexer or the reader but it is interesting and significant that few if any publications follow the standard exactly.

Perhaps the next revision (now under way) should make clearer what recommendations apply specifically to scholarly publications, what recommendations apply to consumer and trade publications, and what recommendations apply to all. At least publishers would know better what was expected of them and not reject the whole standard as unrealistic and unworkable.

The standard has foreseen so many possibilities and makes so many good recommendations that it is hard to find suggestions for additions to it. Two recommendations would in my opinion strengthen the code. Scholarly journals should be printed on acid-free paper. It would be advantageous for other serials as well, but the scholarly journal is intended to be available indefinitely, and surely the additional cost of acid-free paper would be a small one among other costs, and one that libraries would gladly pay for.

This is also the time to push for the adoption of a machine-readable label on the front or back cover of all periodicals. Probably this would take the form of a bar code which would include title and/or ISSN, volume and issue number, and date of the publication. Identification of the publication is now the last labor-intensive problem in serial receiving work in libraries. This feature would eliminate almost all the time-consuming problem-solving and would improve the reliability of records and probably reduce claims and other problem correspondence with publishers. It would allow libraries to use automated serials receiving systems much more efficiently and reliably. The actual work of checking in daily receipts could be cut by 75% or more. A library receiving 1000 periodicals a day, could, if all had bar codes, take account of them all in two and a half hours instead of spending 16 hours keying them into an automated system or 18 hours entering them into a manual file.

If a standard were easy to interpret and relatively painless to follow, it could also be easier to promote. The American National Standards Institute does not advertise its standards individually or promote their adoption and use. It compiles them. Its job is to get leading representatives of the industry together to agree on standards of mutual benefit. Librarians and indexers could promote this standard, however, and should. Through associations, librarians could make a much stronger effort to get the standard into the hands of publishers, many of whom have never seen it or heard of it. If 30% or 40% of the periodicals that now follow the standard loosely or not at all would adhere to it as a guideline and general rule, much expensive staff time would be saved in libraries. The investment of effort would benefit the whole information system in many long-lasting and important ways.

Ironically, it may be too late to have an important effect on the information system if the printed journal declines soon, as some predict. Now is a time when standards need to be developed for microfilm, abstract and electronic journals. Standard vocabulary needs to be adopted, and industry-wide agreement is needed on production quality, sizes, format, terms of access and reproduction privileges. Standardization for electronic journals brings up another important consideration for the new media: bibliographic control.

BIBLIOGRAPHIC CONTROL

The computer giveth and the computer taketh away. New electronic technology is making it possible to index, catalog and retrieve everything—everything that is printed, that is. Electronic technology is giving birth to new forms of publication, in particular the electronic journal, but creating new problems for bibliographic control.

One of the so-called advantages of the electronic journal is that an author can revise a paper after it has been "published." Let's say that A. Buchholz writes a paper on causes of inflation in 1982 and it is published in the *Online Journal of Economics.* In 1983 critic Marbury points out a weakness in Buchholz's paper. Buchholz defends his paper but in late 1983 asks his editor for permission to insert a paragraph elucidating a point only touched on earlier, and eliminating another paragraph that he has come to wish he hadn't written. The revision makes the paper much stronger. Editor Winthrop believes the changes are minor and agrees to them. The revised version defuses Marbury's points. What is reader MacArthur to make of the exchange between Buchholz and Marbury when he reads it in 1985 and looks up Buchholz's "original" paper as it exists in the *Online Journal of Economics*?

Another proposal for the computer is to "unbundle" articles. No longer do papers need to appear with volume and issue numbers and dates with other papers. They can be put into the data base at any time and retrieved at any later time. Of course, parts of papers could be retrieved, just as easily—perhaps a graph or a fact or a finding. But this flexibility exposes the information system to great risks. No fact, finding or graph stands alone. There is research and experimentation behind them, establishing them. Taken out of the context of that background the "facts" are meaningless.

Scientific truth is like a master painting. We need to know its provenance. Separated from its origins and history, it is doubtful. In the context of its proof, it remains true until another researcher can disprove it. The method used by a scholar is as important as his conclusion. Until another researcher can achieve the same results with the same methods, the conclusions cannot be accepted. This is obviously a key point in the scientific community, and the electronic journal must not undercut it.

Since the advent of printing, bibliographic control has been possible because all the copies printed in an edition from a printing press are alike. Describe one and you describe all. The electronic journal is different. It exists not on paper but in a machine—a highly flexible machine that allows its data to be manipulated, changed, added to and deleted. How can we establish bibliographic control over such a medium?

I make the following proposals:

1. Attach date of entry and accession number to each paper in the data base.

2. Create an international standard electronic serial number (ISESN) which would uniquely identify each electronic publication and which would be administered by the International Serials Data System or another international system like it.

3. All retrievals of any part of the data base would bear a bibliographic strip containing author, title, name of publication, ISESN, year and number of paper.

4. Any paper could be revised at any time, but the whole revised article or the changes or additions would be entered as a new paper into the data base without altering the original. The new paper would receive its own unique number, but would be connected by cross reference to the number of the original paper, and vice versa. Those retrieving the paper would get the one requested but would also get a citation to the other which would also be available for retrieval separately.

5. The computer is so flexible that an original paper could be altered despite the above rules. The computer is also subject to failures that can damage or lose part of the data in its memory. To guard against both of these possibilities, each electronic journal would have at least two official depositories for paper copies of each item in the data base. One would be its national library, the Library of Congress, British Library, Biliothèque Nationale or whatever. The other would be a research library that would agree to preserve the paper copies and make them available for study by qualified scholars. The data base would name its depositories as part of its official identification—when users sign on—the counterpart of a printed masthead.

Without these five rules or something similar to them, the electronic journal will not be the true counterpart of the printed journal. If it produces information only, and not the means of verifying the origin of the information, it will not serve as the primary communication medium among scholars.

GOVERNMENT REGULATION

The scholarly enterprise depends upon free investigation of truth and free exchange of information. All governments have a tendency to meddle in these processes, but in the western democracies at least, the freedom of the publishing process is a well-established and hard won principle. By moving into electronic media, publishing enters an area that has a slightly different tradition. The government has a history of regulating electronic communications. Most of this regulation involves the medium, but the monitoring of the content of electronic communication is more pronounced than the monitoring of printed material. The regulation of the medium creates problems. The Communications Act of 1934 created a federal policy that awards monopolies in telecommunications, restricting the entry of new companies that could reduce consumer costs.[6]

What is needed in the U.S. now is a national cooperative effort of publishers, information industry, libraries and government to extend First Amendment protection to electronic media, work out copyright problems, ensure public access to government information, and set up guidelines for use of electromagnetic communication that would require the least possible government involvement. Such a national effort is being studied by the Association of American Publishers.[7] Librarians should unite with them in creating the national consensus and policy that will open up electronic communication to its full potential as a cost saving, reliable, permanent form of information exchange as useful for scholarship as for commerce and entertainment.

FOOTNOTES

1. *The New York Times,* Oct. 20, 1981, pp. 1, 31.

2. H. William Koch, "The Effect of the U.S. Copyright Legislation on Authors, Editors, Publishers, and Librarians," *Journal of Research Communication Studies* 3, no. 1-2 (September 1981): 95.

3. *American National Standard for Periodicals: Format and Arrangement,* ANSI-Z39.1-1977 (New York: American National Standards Institute, 1978), p. [2].

4. Ibid., pp. 12-16.

5. Ibid., p. 2.

6. Cf. Lionel Van Deerlin, "Information Overload; What the Congress and Information Professionals Can Do About It," *Special Libraries* 72 (January 1981): 107.

7. "AAP Ponders Creation of Federal Information Plan," *Publishers Weekly* (June 26, 1981): 21.

8

Further Implications for Libraries

Before we elaborate on some of the implications for libraries raised in the first seven chapters, perhaps we ought to do some simple forecasting based upon what we have learned.

SOME PREDICTIONS

1. It takes no prognosticator to say that we are in a period of economic hardship. Libraries are not building many new buildings and few have budgets that can keep up with the increasing cost of library materials. We should not expect that to change much. There is no reason to expect a surge of new tax monies in the public treasury, even if the national economy improves radically. It just is not the mood of the times.

2. We can expect cuts in the money available to sponsor research. This will affect the amount of research attempted and produced, but it is not likely to reverse the trend of accelerating research and publication. The cutback of grants will hurt publishers directly in cutting out almost entirely the money now used to pay page charges.

3. Balance that with the good news of the enormous progress in the development of computers and various information technologies. We can expect new wonders and improvements on the old ones to come in rapid succession throughout the next decade or so.

4. There will continue to be new serials born, although hard times may cut down on the birth rate, and the death rate may increase to the point that in 10 or 20 years we may expect a net decrease.

5. We can expect the rapid growth of various experimental forms of publication. In 10 years, multiple formats will be the rule, and libraries will have to be able to handle them. Eventually all scholarly serials may be published electronically. For the next few decades, however, we apparently will have a mix of publications: print, microfiche, video, online and perhaps new formats not yet known to us.

125

6. There will continue to be stress between publishers and libraries, and this could become increasingly bitter and hostile. Yet, it must be one of the highest priorities that each cooperate with the other, as each is essential to the other's success.

7. Libraries will continue to cooperate with other libraries in more effective ways. If national legislation does not make a national information system available to fill the needs of libraries, librarians will form what they need through associations, supplemented by services contracted for from information brokers. Such cooperative arrangements will continue to be a bone of contention between publishers and librarians.

8. Publishers may test the legal possibility of refusing to sell to networks or to libraries that are members of networks. Some may try to distribute serials as on-demand publications through commercial information brokers, but not to sell to libraries unless libraries agree to pay a royalty fee for each reading or photocopying of an article. Even if this does not occur, libraries will experience growing competition from information brokers in the supplying of up-to-the-minute information. Information brokers will live on service. If they can supply pertinent information quickly to the people to whom it is valuable, they will be well paid. Most libraries will be unable or unwilling to tailor their information activities to such an extent, but some will do so with the aid of the powerful computers becoming more easily available.

9. The hard times will be reflected by an increasing number of ceased serial titles and publisher failures. Yet the favorable low-capital requirement of the serial publishing business caused by the unique paid-in-advance subscription arrangement will mean that during periods of high interest rates the failure rate of small publishers will be lower than that of other small businesses. Most of the failed publishers will be not-for-profit publishers producing small circulation scholarly journals. Many will die when they lose the sponsorship of university presses, which are themselves in deep trouble. Adroit and aggressive commercial publishers will find a way to survive: by dropping losing titles, by finding ways of cutting costs and increasing income with new formats, particularly the electronic journal, or —in rare cases—by moving out of scholarly publishing into popular entertainment serials.

10. Publishers will exert more pressure on lawmakers and the courts to interpret the copyright law in their favor, by limiting the interpretation of "fair use." Librarians may lose this battle unless they unite in stubborn defense of the traditional interpretation of copyright.

11. The government-sponsored, unrefereed "catch-all" serials—*ERIC Reports* and *NTIS Reports*—could be in trouble with a budget-cutting administration. Librarians need to fight for these services to continue. At a time when other avenues to publishing may become more restricted, they will be needed more than ever. In fact, new unrefereed comprehensive serials may need to be created to serve a similar function in the humanities and the social sciences not now served. If no place for them can be found under government sponsorship, associations of libraries or learned societies might initiate such series on a basis that would make them self-supporting.

12. More scholarly publications will appear in abstract-and-demand or abstract-and-microform form.

13. If the catch-all publications are not lost to budget cutting, there will be sufficient avenues to publish all scholarly research. These publications will fall into classes. Authors will receive more prestige from publishing in the serials with the most subscribers. The class system of publications will look something like this:

> 1. printed on paper, refereed, thousands of personal subscriptions, hundreds of library subscriptions;
> 2. printed on paper, refereed, hundreds of library subscriptions, some personal subscriptions;
> 3. alternative formats—abstract-and-demand, microfiche, electronic, refereed, library subscriptions, few personal subscriptions;
> 4. catch-all serials on microfiche—not refereed, subscriptions by major research libraries, no personal subscriptions.

To a certain extent, this class system already exists. As the new formats gain popularity and develop immediate access to individual scholars, they will rise in prestige. This seems particularly true of the electronic journal. Because it is new, it depends on sophisticated, expensive equipment, and at least in some subject fields it has potential to gain rapid, direct access to the most influential scholars in the field. In such cases, the electronic journal could almost match in prestige the large-volume printed journals in the first class.

14. In response to these trends and developments, libraries will have to:
  A. be efficient in acquiring serials
    1. get all issues subscribed to (order efficiently and claim efficiently)
    2. keep all issues of journals subscribed to (improve security and preservation of collection)
  B. cut back on subscriptions
  C. improve ability to supply serials not owned in a timely fashion
    1. through networking arrangements
      a. quicker identification of and location of titles wanted, and
      b. quicker delivery of copy of document
    2. by subscribing to tear sheet services and on-demand publication services
    3. by keeping up with new technological developments, which will make the library capable of subscribing to electronic journals, or videotext magazines, should such become important avenues for the dissemination of scholarly information.

LIBRARY BUDGETS

Budgets of most libraries have held up remarkably well in the face of the economic downturn of the past three years or so. Recently, however, more academic libraries along with their parent institutions have had to make drastic cuts. Where does a library make cuts to save 5% or 10% of its budget? Normally, cuts in most libraries will occur in the following sequence: first the equipment, then supplies, and finally books and serials. If the cuts go deeper than that and appear to be permanent, then staff positions may be cut. Staff cuts are easy to rationalize if acquisitions budgets are cut to the point that technical service units have little to do, but it is hard for an administrator to give up staff positions, knowing how difficult it is to get them back.

The traditional approach may not be the most appropriate in light of trends in publishing and in libraries. The next decade will be a poor time to have restrictive equipment budgets. OCLC and RLIN have been extremely effective in improving the quality of cataloging. More terminals and related equipment will be needed to take advantage of all the services available from the networks. More equipment will also be needed to use the new, nonprint forms publishing will take.

Libraries that are forced to cut acquisitions may find that some staff cuts are possible in technical services, but may need to add positions in public services. Libraries that can supply 95% of requested materials only need to provide access through interlibrary loans to the other 5%. Libraries that can supply only 90% of requested materials need to provide twice as many interlibrary loans. Unfortunately, interlibrary loans are expensive in staff time.

The use of the computer in public services is also very costly in staff time. A typical online data base search requires a full hour or more of a librarian's time to help just one patron. Doing an online search rather than using printed indexes saves the patron's time, but requires more library staff time. The same is true regarding the use of an online catalog as compared to a card catalog. The time may come when all library patrons know how to use a computer and can find references they need in an online catalog without staff assistance. But a lot of educating and assistance from staff will be needed for a long time before that day arrives.

Cutting budgets is never easy, but these considerations will complicate the task in the next decade or two. To aid in making those decisions, we need more information about the ways libraries are used.

LIBRARY USE STUDIES

Libraries have responded to the need to save money by a lot of commonsense cuts and by a little bit of research into the use of libraries. Studies made all have some points in common: 1) a few library books and serials account for most of the use, and other items are used very little, 2) the most recent books and serials are more likely to circulate than older ones and, therefore, those that are not being read now are not likely to be read in the future, 3) unused books and serials can be put in storage or discarded with very little effect on the way the library is used.

The study by Allen Kent and Associates of the use of materials in the University of Pittsburgh Library (see Chapter 3) has confronted librarians with the question: "Why are we buying these books and journals if no one is using them?" The study has had its critics, both for its assumptions (all circulations of a book are equal, whether to an undergraduate or to a Nobel prize winner) and methodology (dependence on the circulation system record of book use and the sampling method of observation of use of journals in departmental libraries). But its general conclusion that a large number of books and journals in academic libraries are never or rarely used appears irrefutable. Too many other studies verify the conclusion and any doubter with an hour to spare can randomly check books with date due stamps in them in any library and verify that some books circulate a lot, but others circulate rarely or not at all. The Pittsburgh study presents two problems: 1) How can one know *before it is purchased* that a certain book or journal will not be used, and 2) Is it really bad that many library materials don't circulate?

The books and journals that will never be used are a waste of the library's money, but there seems to be no sure way to predict which library acquisitions will turn out to be the unread ones. Reviews may be positive, authors and publishers respectable, and faculty recommendations enthusiastic. The book may still sit. Careful studies of circulation patterns and journal use in a library would help in applying other criteria in collection development. The work of selection would be expensive, however, and might offset the savings in book purchasing.

While reviews and recommendations do not guarantee a book or journal's use, they certainly increase the *probability* of its use. The library with careful selection procedures will still have unread materials, but it should have fewer of them. A particular item that is unused should not be considered a selection error. But a whole category of unused books and journals in the collection should call for evaluation and revision of selection policies.

Selection criteria must be carefully worked out. For instance, books and journals in foreign languages are used relatively infrequently in American university libraries. However, dropping all acquisitions of non-English materials would impoverish the library, and would be indefensible for most academic institutions.

Another approach to book selection would be to spend little staff time on selection by acquiring books in blanket order programs and then in five years discarding the ones that have attracted no interest. A similar approach could be made to serials—purchasing many "on probation" and cancelling them routinely if certain use criteria are not met.

The Value of Less-Read Materials

On the other hand, a library must contemplate its purpose and decide whether circulation statistics measure its programs adequately. A book that is never consulted may be wasted, but a book that was read once in 50 years may have fulfilled its purpose and the library's as much as a book that circulates 20 times a year. The library may have wasted money on a novel that is very popular for a year or two.

It may have spent its money well on a definitive study that makes the library more useful and the university more attractive to scholars and students, even though it is seldom consulted. (For instance, a scholar who is being recruited by a university may be persuaded to accept an appointment because he recognizes the strength of subject collections in the library. He may actually own his own copies and not use the library's, yet their existence in the library is a positive statement to him about the richness of the library and about the university as an environment for research and teaching.)

The assumption that unread serials have been valueless is not necessarily true either. For example, a library school library may collect all of the 40 or so journals and bulletins published by the state and regional library associations in the United States. If 10 were heavily used, 10 more were used some, and the other 20 were used lightly or not at all in a 10-year period, does that mean that the 20 should be cancelled? If they are no longer in the collection, doesn't that weaken the other 20? By having all, the researcher can compare, can know what all are doing, even if some are not doing much. With half of them, even the more important half, the researcher would not know what may have been missed. Indexing cannot cover every aspect that a researcher may find relevant. If cuts must be made, the bulletins with little use would be the first to be cancelled, but the librarian and scholar should recognize that they do have value.

If the library can afford to supply space and maintenance to materials of potential value which have not been used for years, the library gains by retaining them. They hurt no one by being there. On the other hand, lacking items that are needed exacts a penalty of inconvenience to the reader in terms of time and frustration, and perhaps even creates major roadblocks to research.

Without question, most academic libraries should spend more money on added copies of well-used books and journals, even if that is serving undergraduates at the cost of some research support.

The Need to Share Resources

Libraries faced with severe budget cuts will have to find a formula for purchasing the most essential teaching and research materials and depend on networking to provide the rest. Libraries with excellent collections and facilities and not under extreme budget pressure may be able to buy materials for long-range research collection building, but still will need to rely on other libraries through the networks for materials not owned.

Librarians and university administrators will have to decide what the library's future role will be—a major resource library, or a library serving most or much of its users' needs but with fewer unique resources of interest to scholars elsewhere. Both kinds of libraries will serve 95% of their users' needs, but one will continue to act as a collection for gathering and organizing research materials of value to future scholars. The other library will reduce greatly that kind of collecting activity and concentrate its limited resources upon serving the immediate needs of most of its users. The network of libraries of the future will depend on both kinds of libraries.

Each library is different and its community is different. As Harry Kriz observed, "A library must serve the local group of authors, not a subject field. Thus a librarian needs to know what is being used and cited by those who use the library, not what is being cited by those who publish in a particular set of journals." He adds, "In this regard it should be noted that the literature of a specialty must be distinguished from the literature of interest to workers in that specialty."[1]

It cannot be emphasized too strongly that librarians have a compelling obligation to study the actual use of their own libraries. They can use published studies like the Pittsburgh study as guides to methodology and as hypotheses to be built upon, but cannot apply their conclusions directly to another library. Local studies should include interviews with faculty and students. While they may not give definitive answers about future needs, they should help librarians discover weaknesses and strengths they were not aware of which will help meet current and future objectives.

No university library can possibly support all the research needs of all its students and faculty. Neither is it wise for each library to try to anticipate and support a high percentage of the research needs of its faculty. Such materials are used too infrequently to burden every library with them. Some libraries must have them, but not every library.

A large investment must be made soon in the creation of effective and efficient means of supplying material available in one library to users in another library. If this investment is not forthcoming from the federal government, then libraries themselves will have to supply it. Such a network is the guarantee of availability that allows a library to give up the goal of self-sufficiency and collect wisely for maximum local use.

A NATIONAL INFORMATION NETWORK

The declining ability of libraries to buy all the materials needed, or even a significant portion of the publications available, throws more stress on the importance of a national (indeed, international) information network. Such a network must do two things; guarantee the preservation of all useful information, and make possible the efficient and rapid retrieval of that information anywhere in the country.

The success of the British Library Lending Division gave us a model of efficiency and economy that contrasted greatly with the confusion of the American interlibrary loan system. The Council on Library Resources designed an American system based on that model with a national periodical center supporting a national periodical system. It could not achieve a consensus of support among librarians, much less publishers and private information suppliers. It is now dead. No conceivable system could be designed that would be supported by the federal government with a large investment in tax money during these budget-cutting times. An alternative network based on the present strengths of American libraries will have to be devised.

What characteristics will such a network have? The first requirement is bibliographic control. The national cataloging data base being developed in the OCLC, RLIN and WLN systems is the basis for quick identification and location of books and serials in the various libraries. It is creating excellent identification of monographs, but not of articles in journals. The online bibliographic data bases do the latter. They are not yet comprehensive; they are vast, but there still are gaps to be covered. As computer-driven typesetting becomes universal among indexers and abstracters, the information in these data bases will become more complete. The computer networks make this aspect of a national information network workable now.

Where the system fails is with the mechanical labor-dependent means of document delivery. The U.S. mail is a problem, but not nearly so great a problem as the staffing situations in individual libraries. The interlibrary loan program in the OCLC system has bypassed the dependence on the mail for the delivery of requests, and even this small improvement apparently is bringing about a significant increase in interlibrary loan traffic, causing even greater problems for individual library staffs.

The technology which would allow the transmission of documents electronically is available. Several possibilities offer themselves: interactive cable TV, facsimile transmission, or sending and receiving computers with CRT display or printer. Other technological advances that may figure prominently in a future national network are: video disc in interaction with computers, microfacsimile (which transmits images taken directly from microforms), the intelligent copier and the high-speed ink-jet printer.

Any system that depends upon a combination of cooperating repositories of printed materials is likely to be cumbersome and to experience disappointing results. For instance, the average success rate for finding material on the shelf in most academic libraries is between 50% and 60%. Staff time for processing interlibrary loan requests is high, and will almost guarantee that requests will be backlogged, unless the requestor pays a charge of $5 or more. The better the service a library gives, the more requests it will receive. The only way to discourage the requests is to charge fees or to take a long time in processing them.

If in the future much or most information requested by one library from another or from a commercial information provider is already in machine-readable form, the system can allow almost instantaneous response and therefore will have a large capacity for handling requests. As long as it must be retrieved physically from shelves or files, and taken to a machine to record or transmit or copy, the system will tend to be inefficient. The most efficient way to organize such a mechanical and labor-dependent system is to centralize it, which is politically impossible at present. Consequently, we recognize that the network of information will struggle with frustrating problems for quite some time, until technology or politics rescues us.

A NATIONAL NETWORK—A PROPOSAL

I propose an interim solution to the need for a national information network along the following lines:

1. Expect little or no government money.

2. Use a membership plan to create the capital for the investment needed for equipment and collections.

3. Create a central collection of the most-used periodicals. Start small—with current subscriptions to perhaps 5000 titles. Add titles and back volumes as use indicates and money becomes available. Except for this small core of titles, rely mostly on existing collections in member libraries. Perhaps an existing library could house the central collection. The best choice for such a center might be the Center for Research Libraries (CRL), which now operates on the same sort of dues income from member libraries. Probably no library

could afford to belong to CRL *and* such a network, so it would be advantageous for all if CRL were transformed rather than continuing to operate in competition to a new organization.

4. Pay royalties to publishers on all photocopies from the central collection, but not from member libraries. This would probably generate in the neighborhood of $1 million in fees for publishers.

5. Create an efficient center capable of responding to a request with a mailed photocopy in 24 hours. Work for the same sort of response from member libraries.

6. Use the investment capital for initial collection, staff and the best equipment—with computer record keeping and high-speed copiers.

Development of the System

7. Be ready to use computer-controlled video discs, high-speed printers or similar technology as it becomes available and capable of providing quick access to and reproduction of individual articles in serials in the collection.

8. Use capital to create the capability for facsimile transmission when it is feasible. This will require not only sophisticated equipment at the center, but sending and receiving units in member libraries.

9. Use the OCLC ILL system or a similar system to request loans and photocopies by electronic means, not by mail. Requests for books and journal articles and other materials could be sent within the system to any of the member libraries.

Charges

10. Charges could be calculated on a sliding scale based on enrollment, collection, staff size and other pertinent criteria, including perhaps previously reported ILL activity. Charges should not be made on a per-transaction basis, which would tend to discourage use of the system. Libraries may be tempted to pass charges on to users or restrict loans to certain classes of patrons. Charges by other categories may encourage libraries to promote system use to get more value for money invested.

11. Libraries that loaned to other libraries or received requests for loans at certain rates would receive money from the system to help pay for their costs. For instance, a library that loaned 10,000 items might receive $10,000 and a library that loaned 20,000 or more $20,000, while the library loaning 3000 would receive nothing. While such an arrangement might not pay all the costs incurred in lending materials, it could compensate libraries for some of their costs and make it possible for major libraries to drop interlibrary loan fees and to join the network.

12. Membership fees might run from a maximum of $30,000 down to $5000 for public, research and academic libraries, with smaller fees for small public libraries. Special libraries

might pay on the basis of service contracts using formulas similar to selective dissemination of information service fees.

13. It should be feasible for such a system to be self-supporting once it has been established. Start-up costs are a different matter. How does a library whose budget has just been trimmed by $200,000 come up with an extra $30,000 network membership fee? Let three employees go or cancel another 60 subscriptions? Once a library has such a fee established in its budget, it will be much easier to justify continuing it. What is needed then, are the strong incentives of matching grants to initiate participation by librarians. Since the federal government is not likely to help significantly, librarians must persuade foundations to furnish much of the capital.

14. The most difficult task in creating the network will be to achieve a consensus of librarians, publishers and information brokers on the value of the system and its design. With or without federal legislation to initiate the system, general agreement among these groups will be politically crucial. Probably the way to achieve it is for the design of the system to come from one or two associations, for instance, the Association of Research Libraries and the Council on Library Resources. Then, ratification of a sort must be won from other groups: the National Commission on Libraries and Information Science, the American Library Association, the American Society for Information Science, the Canadian Library Association, the Association of American Universities, the Information Industries Association and the Association of American Publishers, or as many of these as possible.

15. Such a network should be governed by a board elected from a users council which represents each participating library.

The proposal I am making is reminiscent of the Arthur D. Little report, representing something of a compromise between his System A (the present system unsubsidized and naturally developing without overall planning) and System C (a subsidized distributed network emphasizing sophisticated technology to use more efficiently the collections already in existence).[2]

PRESERVATION

Every library has to be concerned to some extent with the preservation of its materials. Some measures are taken to keep collections safe from thieves and mutilators. Books and journals are handled, bound, stored and mended in ways that are intended to maintain their useful life in the library. Most American librarians have not been ultra concerned about these matters, however. They have accepted the need to replace "missing" books as the price of doing business in open shelf libraries that allow readers to have the most favorable interaction with books and serials. American librarians have decried the quality of paper used in the manufacturing of books, but few have known what to do about the problem, and very few libraries have adequate programs for restoring and preserving fragile materials.

The Need to Combat Deterioration

We must view the urgency of preservation in a new light, however, if our predictions of the future prove accurate. If we may expect the printing of books and journals to decline, the volumes now in libraries will quickly become more difficult to replace. And if libraries become more committed to an integrated national network, each will have a responsibility not only to its own constituents, but also to those of the other libraries to keep those unique materials available to all. One of the biggest changes in American libraries will have to be an increased emphasis on preserving library materials.

Manufacturing processes used since the mid-nineteenth century produce cheaper paper with a short life expectancy. The paper is strong enough and has good quality, but the process leaves acid in the paper that works with oxygen to break down the fibres. The warmer the temperature, the faster the breakdown occurs. Soon the paper has turned brown and has lost all flexibility and strength. Instead of bending, it breaks, and given a few years, will shatter and crumble.

Millions of volumes of books and serials are turning to dust on the shelves of American libraries. Columbia University announced in 1980 that 30% of its collection was in danger of irreversible deterioration and that $34 million would be required to preserve those materials.[3] Few libraries have even surveyed their collections to discover what the damage is, but all are suffering from it. Controlled humidity and cool temperatures slow the deterioration, but do not reverse it. A process developed by William J. Barrow and funded by the Council on Library Resources alters the acid content to produce a more durable paper. Other expensive, labor-intensive procedures must be taken with paper that has already become fragile.

To put this problem in perspective, let us assume that an author, say Stephen Crane, wrote some sketches and short stories that appeared anonymously in local newspapers in New Jersey while he was an unknown journalist. Scholars have combed collections of those papers, looking for items to add to the canon, but may not have found them all. It is imperative that copies of those newspapers survive, and if at all possible, in the original, not in reprinted or microfilmed format. It is not necessary that 50 copies of each newspaper survive, although it would certainly be nice to have more than one copy. This preservation should not be a priority of only the Montclair Public Library, which happens to own one of the old newspapers. International scholarship needs those papers, and a way should be found to insure their preservation for all.

The above illustration will be multiplied many times by the network interdependency that libraries will have, and intensified as materials crumble and replacement copies of printed books and serials become harder to find. Somehow, a nationally or internationally coordinated effort must be made to preserve printed works. As much or more effort must be put into this program as is put into coordinating the acquisitions and cataloging of significant works.

Deteriorating paper is one problem. The film medium used to "preserve" materials on microfilm is made with various formulas, some of them at a cost that is making them out of reach for most libraries. But even the best quality microfilm has shown signs of breaking down, especially if not stored in absolutely perfect conditions, which few libraries can provide. Ironically, it may be standard practice now for libraries to purchase newspapers on microfilm for permanent storage, and to throw away the newsprint originals, only to find that the film has a life expectancy no longer than the paper. Much more investigation must be made into the permanency of microfilm if it is to be a major tool in the effort to save library collections.*

Loss Through Theft and Mutilation

A third problem is presented by the destructive behavior of the users of libraries. Security in libraries is not good, but librarians may not be as alarmed by it as they should be. To a department store manager, the loss of 2% of the inventory is a loss of profit. He may accept it as the price of doing business in a self-service operation, and worth the risk. He can also add the cost of losses to his prices.

A 2% loss of inventory in a library is quite a different thing. It is the permanent loss of a collection that has been acquired at great expense and was intended to remain in the library forever or at least for many years. Lost books and serials can only partially be replaced. The more valuable the item, the less likely it will be available on the used-book market. Unfortunately, the people who steal books from libraries want the most valuable or most-demanded ones, so they denude the collections of their best and most-used books.

Libraries have spent thousands of dollars on sophisticated electronic security systems and even uniformed guards, and these measures are effective in saving collections. Yet more needs to be done, if libraries take seriously their roles in a national information network of the future. It may be that libraries will have to rethink their dedication to the open-shelf ideal. Serials often are treated differently from books in the circulation policy of academic libraries. Bound periodicals rarely circulate, while almost all books do.

This difference in treatment shows up in the ways materials are mistreated. Books are stolen, but periodicals are mutilated. The library that is concerned about preserving its collections may examine all policies concerning its various materials, and may conclude that books and serials should not be treated differently. Or, the conclusion may be the opposite: the treatment of books and serials should be more divergent than it is. For instance, it may not make good sense to shelve periodicals by call number interfiled with books. Perhaps the most compelling problem that results from interfiling in the stacks is the lack of supervision of periodical use. If periodicals were housed in a separate collection, and were used in a reading room with a staff supervisor, most mutilation would not occur. An increased need for preservation in a future network system may lead libraries to take these or other precautions to improve their ability to safeguard their collections.

---

*For a comprehensive treatment of preservation techniques and issues, see *The Preservation Challenge: A Guide to Conserving Library Materials,* by Carolyn Clark Morrow (White Plains, NY: Knowledge Industry Publications, Inc., 1982).

HUMAN RESOURCES

The changing environment in libraries places a new emphasis on the importance of staff. Experienced librarians need training to be able to adapt to new techniques. Clerical staff positions may need to be upgraded to require library and computer skills. Staff may need to be reassigned, perhaps putting more clerical positions in technical services and more professional positions in public services. Computers will also change the work environment for many library staff members.

Michael Gorman has become the recognized spokesman for a point of view that traditional serials departments should be done away with.[4] Gorman points out that work with the manual serials records files around which serials departments are presently organized is unrewarding, demanding and frustrating. We really should not expect people to have to work under such conditions, doing what is practically coolie labor. The low pay and low recognition of our serials check-in clerks are reflections of the thankless kind of jobs they perform.

The computer can change that. It will demand higher-level skills of the personnel and do the most irritating, boring work (systematic searching for claims needed, writing or typing out the claims, alphabetizing stacks of mail) and perhaps eventually recognize and check in each issue by machine-readable bar codes. It should free staff to do more crucial and interesting work, solving problems. At present, automation costs are high and check-in capabilities slow, but these problems will surely be overcome in the future.

I do not believe the computer will eliminate printed serials, nor will it eliminate the need for serials staff, or a specialized unit of experts to handle serials.

THE ELECTRONIC LIBRARY

It is surely coming, but whether in 1995 or 2095 is a question of some interest. F.W. Lancaster, in numerous books and articles, has warned librarians of the changes that are coming.[5] If libraries are not ready for new forms of communication, warns Lancaster, they will be passed by. Consumers of information in the age we are entering will get their information elsewhere, and libraries will become museums of old information.

According to Roistacher, the electronic journal naturally belongs in research libraries.[6] In libraries users will get the assistance they need, and journals will find the wide audience they need if they are to fulfill their mission.

The electronic journal and the library need each other, just as the printed journal and the library need each other. But many problems need to be overcome—questions of price, methods of acquisition and payment, copyright and rights of reproduction, sharing among libraries and bibliographic control—before it can be asserted with confidence that libraries will have electronic journals and that such journals will be viable forms of scholarly communication.

On the other hand, it will be many years and perhaps decades before printed publications will cease to be produced. It will be even longer before libraries can give up their present collections of printed materials. Some special libraries may be able to furnish electronic information only, but most academic and public libraries will always need most of their printed collections. There is no prospect of converting the vast accumulations of printed materials in libraries to electronic forms retrospectively. Despite declining use rates, libraries will want to keep many older printed materials as long as historians, scholars of literature and students still need to refer to them. Present and foreseeable technology do not appear to offer means of publishing literary work, history and other important forms of writing.

CONCLUSIONS

This chapter began with some forecasting. Let's end with some more. Some libraries will be aptly described as electronic in a few years. Some libraries will possibly resist the new formats and will become museums of printed artifacts or close down altogether. Most libraries will have mixed collections, however, for the next few decades, with information in paper, microfilm, audiovisual and electronic forms.

The computer of the future will have the capacity to store and retrieve information in ways we can scarcely imagine. Nevertheless, for many years most libraries will stumble along under less than ideal conditions. Both library staff and the public will adjust and learn new skills to find information, but retain the old methods too. Soon the alternative format serial will be commonplace, but as long as there are libraries that purchase printed materials, printed serials will persist. Libraries will acquire and manage serials, in whatever format they are published.

FOOTNOTES

1. Harry M. Kriz, "Subscriptions vs. Books in a Constant Dollar Budget," *College and Research Libraries* (39):2 (March 1978):106.

2. *A Comparative Evaluation of Alternative Systems for the Provision of Effective Access to Periodical Literature,* by Arthur D. Little, Co. (Washington, DC: National Commission on Libraries and Information Science, 1979): II-2 to V-21.

3. Norman D. Stevens, "The Preservation Crisis," *Library Issues: Briefings for Academic Officers* (supplement to *The Journal of Academic Librarianship*) (1):2 (November 1980):290.

4. Michael Gorman, "Role of Serials Control in Future Library Organization," presentation at Conference on Serials Automation, Acquisitions and Inventory Control (Milwaukee: September 4, 5, 1980), 60-minute sound cassette from *Information Yield.*

5. F.W. Lancaster, *Toward Paperless Information Systems* (New York: Academic Press, 1978); "Whither Libraries? or Wither Libraries," *College and Research Libraries* (39):5 (September 1978): 345-357; "The Role of the Library in an Electronic Society," in Clinic on Library Applications of Data Processing (proceedings, 1980), *The Role of the Library in an Electronic Society* (Urbana: University of Illinois Graduate School of Library Science, 1980), pp. 162-191; "The Future of the Library in the Age of Telecommunications," in *Telecommunications and Libraries: A Primer for Librarians and Information Managers* (White Plains, NY: Knowledge Industry Publications, Inc., 1981), pp. 137-156; F.W. Lancaster and Donald W. King, "Libraries and the Transfer of Information," in *Telecommunications and Libraries,* pp. 7-21.

6. Richard Roistacher, "The Virtual Journal: Reaching the Reader," in Clinic on Library Applications of Data Processing (proceedings, 1980), *The Role of the Library in an Electronic Society,* op cit., pp. 19, 20.

Selected Bibliography

Allen, Walter C., ed. *Serial Publications in Large Libraries.* (Allerton Park Institute no. 16) Urbana, IL: University of Illinois Graduate School of Library Science, 1970.

American National Standard for Periodicals: Format and Arrangement. (ANSI Z39.1-1977) New York: American National Standards Institute, 1978.

Asser, P.N. "Some Trends in Journal Subscriptions," *Scholarly Publishing,* vol. 10 (April 1979) 279-86.

Ballard, Tom. "Public Library Networking: Neat, Plausible, Wrong," *Library Journal,* vol. 107 (April 1, 1982) 679-83.

Battin, Patricia. "Libraries, Computers, and Scholarship," *Wilson Library Bulletin,* vol. 56 (April 1982) 580-83.

Blackwell's Periodicals Conference, 2nd, Trinity College, Oxford, 23-24 March, 1977. Proceedings: *Economics of Serials Management.* edited by David P. Woodworth. Loughborough, England: Serials Group, 1977.

Bosseau, Don. *University of California, San Diego Serials System.* (Computerized Serials System Series, vol. 1, issue 2) Tempe, AZ: The Larc Association, 1973.

Broad, William J. "Journals: Fearing the Electronic Future," *Science,* vol. 216 (May 28, 1982) 964-68.

———— "The Publishing Game: Getting More for Less," *Science,* vol. 211 (March 13, 1981) 1137-39.

Brown, Eleanor Frances. *Cutting Library Costs: Increasing Productivity and Raising Revenues.* Metuchen, NJ: Scarecrow Press, 1979.

Brown, Norman B. and Jane Phillips. "Price Indexes for 1981, U.S. Periodicals and Serial Services," *Library Journal,* vol. 106 (July 1981) 1387-93.

Buckland, Michael K. *Book Availability and the Library User.* New York: Pergamon Press, 1975.

Butler, Meredith. "Copyright and Reserve Books—What Librarians Are Doing," *College and Reserve Libraries News,* vol. 39 (May 1978) 125-29.

Clinic on Library Applications of Data Processing, 1972. *Applications of On-Line Computers to Library Problems.* Urbana, IL: University of Illinois Graduate School of Library Science, 1973.

Clinic on Library Applications of Data Processing, 1979. *The Role of the Library in an Electronic Society.* Urbana, IL: University of Illinois Graduate School of Library Science, 1980.

Council on Library Resources. *A National Periodicals Center Technical Development Plan.* Washington, DC: Council on Library Resources, 1978.

Davinson, D.E. *The Periodicals Collection.* Rev. and Enl. Ed. London: A. Deutsch, 1978.

DeGennaro, Richard. "Austerity, Technology, and Resource Sharing: Research Libraries in the Future," *Library Journal,* vol. 100 (May 15, 1975) 917-23.

_____ "Copyright, Resource Sharing, and Hard Times: A View from the Field," *American Libraries,* vol. 8 (September 1977) 430-35.

_____ "Escalating Journal Prices: Time to Fight Back," *American Libraries,* vol. 8 (February 1977) 69-74.

_____ "Libraries and Networks in Transition: Problems and Prospects for the 1980's," *Library Journal,* vol. 106 (May 15, 1981) 1045-49.

_____ "Research Libraries Enter the Information Age," *Library Journal,* vol. 104 (November 15, 1979) 2405-10.

_____ "Wanted, a Minicomputer Serials Control System," *Library Journal,* vol. 102 (April 15, 1977) 878-79.

Dodson, James T. and Laurence Miller. "Soaring Journal Costs: A Cooperative Solution," *Library Journal,* vol. 105 (September 15, 1980) 1793-95.

Economics of Scientific Publications. Washington, DC: Council of Biology Editors, 1973.

Farewell to Alexandria; Solutions to Space, Growth, and Performance Problems of Libraries. edited by Daniel Gore. Westport, CT: Greenwood Press, 1976.

Fayollat, James. "On-Line Serials Control in a Large Biomedical Library: Part 1. Description of the System," *Journal of the American Society for Information Science,* vol. 23 (September 1972) 318-22.

Featheringham, Tom R. "Computerized Conferencing and Human Communication," *IEEE Transactions on Professional Communication,* vol. PC-20 (December 1977) 207-13.

———— "Paperless Publishing and Potential Institutional Change," *Scholarly Publishing,* vol. 13 (October 1981) 19-24.

Fry, Bernard M. and Herbert S. White. *Economics and Interaction of the Publisher-Library Relationship in the Production and Use of Scholarly and Research Journals.* (NTIS PB249 108) Washington, DC: National Science Foundation Office of Information Service, 1975.

———— "Impact of Economic Pressures on American Libraries and Their Decisions Concerning Scholarly and Research Journal Acquisition and Retention," *Library Acquisitions: Practice and Theory,* vol. 3 (1979) 153-237.

———— *Publishers and Libraries: A Study of Scholarly and Research Journals.* Lexington, MA: D.C. Heath & Co., 1976.

Fussler, H.H. and J.L. Simon. *Patterns in the Use of Books in Large Research Libraries.* Chicago: University of Chicago Press, 1969.

The Future of Publishing by Scientific and Technical Societies: Proceedings of the Seminar Held in Luxembourg by the Commission of the European Communities with the Co-operation of the European Science Foundation, April 3-4, 1978. Luxembourg: Commission of the European Communities, 1978.

Gabriel, Michael R. *The Microform Revolution in Libraries.* Greenwich, CT: JAI Press, 1980.

Garfield, Eugene. "Citation Analysis as a Tool in Journal Evaluation," *Science,* vol. 178 (November 3, 1972) 471-79.

Garvey, William D. *Communication: The Essence of Science; Facilitating Information Exchange among Librarians, Scientists, Engineers, and Students.* New York: Pergamon Press, 1979.

Goehlert, Robert. "Journal Use Per Monetary Unit: A Reanalysis of Use Data," *Library Acquisitions: Practice and Theory,* vol. 3 (1979) 91-98.

Golden, Susan. "Online Serials Circulation in a Library Network," *Wilson Library Bulletin,* vol. 56 (March 1982) 511-15.

Gore, Daniel. "Curbing the Growth of Academic Libraries," *Library Journal,* vol. 106 (November 1, 1981) 2183-87.

Gorman, Michael. "On Doing Away with Technical Services Departments," *American Libraries,* vol. 10 (July/August 1979) 435-37.

Gorman, Michael and Robert H. Burger. "Serial Control in a Developed Machine System," *The Serials Librarian,* vol. 5 (fall 1980) 13-26.

Guillaume, Jeanne. "Computer Conferencing and the Development of an Electronic Journal," *Canadian Journal of Information Science,* vol. 5 (May 1980) 21-29.

Haas, Warren J. "Research Libraries and the Dynamics of Change," *Scholarly Publishing,* vol. 11 (April 1980) 195-202.

Hayes, Robert M. "On-Line Microfiche Catalogs," *Journal of Micrographics,* vol. 13 (March/April 1980) 15-33, 58-63.

Heilprin, L.B. "The Library Community at a Technological and Philosophical Crossroads: Necessary and Sufficient Conditions for Survival," *Journal of the American Society for Information Science,* vol. 31 (November 1980) 389-97.

Hickey, Thomas. "The Journal in the Year 2000," *Wilson Library Bulletin,* vol. 56 (December 1981) 256-59.

Houghton, B. *Scientific Periodicals: Their Historical Development, Characteristics and Control.* London: Clive Bingley, 1975.

Huff, William H. "The National Periodicals Center," *Catholic Library World,* vol. 52 (February 1981) 276-79.

IEEE Conference on Scientific Journals, 3rd. "Proceedings," *IEEE Transactions on Professional Communication,* vol. PC-20 (1977).

International Conference of Scientific Editors, 2nd, "Proceedings," *Journal of Research Communication Studies,* vol. 3, nos. 1-3, (September and December 1981).

Jacob, Mary Ellen. "A National Interlibrary Loan Network: The OCLC Approach," *Bulletin of the American Society for Information Science,* vol. 5 (June 1979) 24-25.

"Journal Costs Alarming Scholars," *Chronicle of Higher Education,* vol. 11 (November 17, 1975).

Kamens, Harry H. "OCLC Serials Control Subsystem: A Case Study," *The Serials Librarian,* vol. 3 (fall 1978) 43-55.

Kent, Allen, et al. *Use of Library Materials, The University of Pittsburgh Study.* New York: Marcel Dekker, Inc., 1979.

King Research, Inc. *A Chart Book of Indicators of Scientific and Technical Communication in the United States.* Washington, DC: National Science Foundation, Division of Information Science and Technology, 1977.

———— Interim Report: *Analysis of Library Photocopying and Feasibility Test of Proposed Royalty Payment Mechanisms and Minitex Data Analysis.* Rockville, MD: King Research, Inc., 1977.

King, Donald W. *The Journal in Scientific Communication: The Roles of Authors, Publishers, Librarians, and Readers in a Vital System.* Rockville, MD: King Research, Inc., 1979.

King, Donald W., et al. *Library Photocopying in the United States: With Implications for the Development of a Copyright Royalty Payment Mechanism.* Rockville, MD: King Research, Inc., 1977.

———— *Statistical Indicators of Scientific and Technical Communication (1960-1980).* vol. 1-5, Rockville, MD: King Research, Inc., 1976-1979.

King, Donald W., Brigitte L. Kenney and F.W. Lancaster, et al. *Telecommunications and Libraries: A Primer for Librarians and Information Managers.* White Plains, NY: Knowledge Industry Publications, Inc., 1981.

King, Donald W. and Nancy Roderer. *Systems Analysis of Scientific and Technical Communication in the United States: The Electronic Alternative to Communication through Paper-Based Journals.* Rockville, MD; King Research, Inc., 1978.

Kochen, Manfred. "Technology and Communication in the Future," *Journal of the American Society for Information Science,* vol. 32 (March 1981) 148-57.

Kriz, Harry M. "Subscriptions vs. Books in a Constant Dollar Budget," *College and Research Libraries,* vol. 39 (March 1978) 105-09.

Kronick, David A. "Goodbye to Farewells: Resource Sharing and Cost Sharing," *The Journal of Academic Librarianship,* vol. 8 (July 1982) 132-36.

———— *A History of Scientific and Technical Periodicals; The Origins and Development of the Scientific and Technical Press 1665-1790.* 2nd ed. Metuchen, NJ: Scarecrow Press, 1976.

Kuney, J.H. "The Role of Microforms in Journal Publication," *Journal of Chemical Documentation,* vol. 12 (May 1972) 76-78.

Lancaster, F.W. "The Future of Indexing and Abstracting Services," *Journal of the American Society for Information Science,* vol. 33 (May 1982) 115-23.

———— *Toward Paperless Information Systems.* New York: Academic Press, 1978.

Larc Institute on Automated Serials System, St. Louis, May 24, 25, 1973. *Proceedings.* Tempe, AZ: The Larc Association, 1974.

Lawrence, John Shelton and Bernard Timberg. *Fair Use and Free Inquiry, Copyright Law and the New Media.* Norwood, NJ: Ablex, 1980.

Lerner, Rita, and Colin K. Mick and Daniel Callahan. *Database Searching and Document Delivery Via Communications Satellite.* New York: American Institute of Physics, 1980.

Lieberman Research, Inc. *How and Why People Buy Magazines, a National Study of the Consumer Market for Magazines.* Port Washington, NY: Publishers Clearing House, 1977.

Line, Maurice B. and D.N. Wood. "The Effect of Large-Scale Photocopying Service on Journal Sales," *Journal of Documentation,* vol. 31 (December 1975) 234-45.

Little, Arthur D. and Co. *A Comparative Evaluation of Alternative Systems for the Provision of Effective Access to Periodical Literature.* Washington, DC: National Commission on Libraries and Information Science, 1979.

Lowell, Gerald R. "Periodical Prices 1979-81 Update," *Serials Librarian,* vol. 5 (spring 1981) 91-99.

Machlup, Fritz, Kenneth W. Leeson and Associates. *Information through the Printed Word.* vol. 1-4. New York: Praeger Publishers, 1978-80.

Maxin, J.A. "Periodical Use and Collection Development," *College and Research Libraries,* vol. 40 (May 1979) 248-53.

Meadows, A.J., ed., *Development of Science Publishing in Europe.* Amsterdam: Elsevier Science Publishers, 1980.

_____ *The Scientific Journal.* London: Aslib, 1979.

Meadows, Jack, et al. "What is the Future for New Research Journals in the 1980's? A Discussion," *Journal of Research Communication Studies,* vol. 2 (November 1980) 137-47.

Mott, Frank Luther. *A History of American Magazines.* vol. 1, 2. Cambridge: Harvard University Press, 1957.

Murfin, Marjorie E. "The Myth of Accessibility: Frustration and Failure in Retrieving Periodicals," *Journal of Academic Librarianship,* vol. 6 (March 1980) 16-19.

National Commission on Libraries and Information Science. Task Force on a National Periodicals System. *Effective Access to the Periodical Literature: A National Program.* Washington, DC: National Commission on Libraries and Information Science, 1972.

National Commission on New Technological Uses of Copyrighted Works. *Final Report, July 31, 1978.* Washington, DC: Library of Congress, 1979.

"National Interlibrary Loan Code," in *American Library Directory, 1981.* New York: R.R. Bowker Co., 1981. 1699-1700.

National Technical Architecture Group. *Message Delivery System for the National Library and Information Service Network: General Requirements.* edited by David C. Hartmann. (Network Planning Paper, No. 4) Washington, DC: Library of Congress, 1978.

The On-Line Revolution in Libraries, edited by Allen Kent and Thomas J. Galvin. New York: Marcel Dekker, Inc., 1978.

Osborn, Andrew W. *Serial Publications, Their Place and Treatment in Libraries.* 3rd ed. Chicago: American Library Association, 1980.

Palmour, Vernon E., Marcia C. Bellassai and Robert R.V. Wiederkehr. *Costs of Owning, Borrowing, and Disposing of Periodical Publications.* Arlington, VA: The Public Research Institute, 1977.

Palmour, Vernon E. *A Study of the Characteristics, Costs, and Magnitude of Interlibrary Loans in Academic Libraries.* Westport, CT: Greenwood Press, 1972.

Pitkin, Gary M. *Serials Automation in the United States: a Bibliographical History.* Metuchen, NJ: Scarecrow Press, 1976.

Price, Derek DeSolla. *Little Science, Big Science.* New York: Columbia University Press, 1963.

The Print Publisher in an Electronic World. White Plains, NY: Knowledge Industry Publications, Inc., 1981.

Quirk, Dantia and Patricia Whitestone. *The Shrinking Library Dollar.* White Plains, NY: Knowledge Industry Publications, Inc., 1982.

Roderer, Nancy K. and Colleen G. Schell. *Statistical Indicators of Scientific and Technical Communication Worldwide.* Rockville, MD: King Research, Inc., 1977.

Roughton, Michael. "OCLC Serials Records: Errors, Omissions, and Dependability," *Journal of Academic Librarianship*, vol. 5 (January 1980) 316-21.

Rowland, J.F.B. "Synopsis Journals as Seen by Their Authors," *Journal of Documentation*, vol. 37 (June 1981) 69-76.

Sager, Donald J. "A National Periodicals Center: Too Limited a Goal," *American Libraries*, vol. 10 (September 1979) 465-67.

Scholarly Communications, the Report of the National Enquiry. Baltimore: Johns Hopkins University Press, 1979.

Scholars and Their Publishers. edited by Weldon A. Kefauver. New York: Modern Language Association of America, 1977.

Serials Automation for Acquisition and Inventory Control. edited by William Gray Potter and Arlene Farber Sirkin. Chicago: American Library Association, 1981.

Shotwell, Roloyn. "Books on Demand — 2: What's Happening Now," *Publishers Weekly*, vol. 219 (June 5, 1981) 50-52.

Singleton, Alan. "The Electronic Journal and Its Relatives," *Scholarly Publishing*, vol. 13 (October 1981) 3-18.

Stevens, Norman D. "Library Networks and Resource Sharing in the United States: An Historical and Philosophical Overview," *Journal of the American Society for Information Science*, vol. 31 (November 1980) 405-12.

Suprenant, Tom. "Future Libraries: The Electronic Environment," *Wilson Library Bulletin,* vol. 56 (January 1982) 336-41.

Terrant, Seldon W. *Evaluation of a Dual Journal Concept.* Washington, DC: National Science Foundation Division of Science Information, 1977.

Trueswell, R.W. "Determining the Optimal Number of Volumes of a Library's Core Collection," *Libri,* vol. 16 (1966) 49-60.

_____ "Some Behavioral Patterns of Library Users: the 80:20 Rule," *Wilson Library Bulletin,* vol. 43 (January 1969) 450-61.

Turoff, Murray and Tom Featheringham. "Libraries and Communication-Information Technology," *Catholic Library World,* vol. 50 (April 1979) 368-73.

Warner, Edward S. and Anita L. Anker. "Faculty Perceived Needs for Serial Titles: Measurement for Purposes of Collection Development and Management," *Serials Librarian,* vol. 4 (spring 1980) 295-300.

Warner, Edward S. "Impact of Interlibrary Access to Periodicals on Subscription Continuation/Cancellation Decision Making," *Journal of the American Society for Information Science,* vol. 32 (March 1981) 93-95.

Weber, David C. "A Century of Cooperative Programs among Academic Libraries," *College and Research Libraries,* vol. 37 (May 1976) 205-21.

Weil, S. "Survey of the Use and Cost of Scientific Journals," *Special Libraries,* vol. 70 (April 1979) 182-89.

White, Herbert S. and Bernard M. Fry. *The Impact of Periodical Availability on Individual and Library Subscription Placement and Cancellation.* (NTIS PB80-111 883) Washington, DC: National Technical Information Service, 1979.

White, Herbert S. "Publishers, Libraries, and Costs of Journal Subscriptions in Times of Funding Retrenchment," *Library Quarterly,* vol 46 (October 1976) 350-77.

Willmering, William J. "On-Line Centralized Serials Control," *Serials Librarian,* vol. 1 (spring 1977) 243-49.

Williams, Gordon, et al. *Library Cost Models: Owning Versus Borrowing Serial Publications.* Washington, DC: National Science Foundation, 1968.

Williams, Gordon. "Interlibrary Loan Service in the United States," in *Essays on Information and Libraries.* (festschrift for Donald Urquhart). London: Clive Bingley, 1975. 193-206.

Wooton, C.B. "The Growth of the Literature and the Implications for Library Storage and Serials," *BLL Review,* vol. 4 (April 1976) 41-46.

Index

ABOUT THE AUTHOR

David C. Taylor is undergraduate librarian, University of North Carolina, Chapel Hill. Previous positions were as serials librarian, Michigan State University; interlibrary loan and reference librarian, University of Rhode Island; and circulation librarian, Union Theological Seminary. Mr. Taylor was editor and publisher of *Title Varies,* a newsletter on serials issues, from 1973 to 1980. A graduate of Phillips University, he holds a B.D. (ministry) from the University of Chicago and an M.A. (library science) from Columbia University.